THE WORLD'S GREATEST TOY TRAIN MAKER

Insiders Remember Lionel

Roger Carp

KALMBACH
BOOKS

Printed in the United States of America

97 98 99 00 01 02 03 04 05 06   10 9 8 7 6 5 4 3 2 1

For more information, visit our website at
http://www.kalmbach.com

Publisher's Cataloging-in-Publication
(Provided by Quality Books, Inc.)

The world's greatest toy train maker : insiders
   remember Lionel / [edited by] Roger Carp.

      p.   cm.

      1. Lionel Corporation—History. 2. Railroads—Models
—History.   I. Carp, Roger.

TF197.W67 1997   338.7'62919'0973
                               QBI97-40438

Book design: Kristi Ludwig

CONTENTS

ACKNOWLEDGMENTS

The notion that we, who collect and operate Lionel trains today, are heirs to the company's legacy, is one that nearly all former employees and their descendants have impressed upon me. I am grateful for the cooperation and trust these men and women have provided. Without the information and materials they have shared, our understanding and appreciation of Lionel and its history would be small indeed.

Similarly, certain individuals who collect paper and memorabilia related to Lionel have advanced my research. It's a pleasure to be able to thank Joe Algozzini, Ron Antonelli, David Dansky, William Mekalian, Lou Niederlander, Robert Osterhoff, Ed Prendeville, and Donald Simonini for showing me items in their collections. We've enjoyed sharing thoughts about Lionel and hypothesizing about why it succeeded and where it fell short. I value their friendship and look forward to learning from them for many years to come.

At Kalmbach Publishing Co., my research and writing have been encouraged by a number of colleagues. Dick Christianson and Russ Larson have supported my efforts to locate and interview former Lionelers for several years. Dick, Mary Algozin, Sybil Sosin, and Terry Spohn in the Books Department read and commented on various chapters, as did Terry Thompson of *Classic Toy Trains*. Kristi Ludwig skillfully designed the entire book; Chris Becker, Darla Evans, and Jim Forbes took the handsome portraits; Jennifer Gaertner supervised production; and Julie LaFountain handled an array of editorial tasks with grace and patience. For their advice and cooperation, I am very grateful.

Before letting nine of the former Lionel employees that I've interviewed tell their stories, I'd like to share one of my own, a story that explains my reason for having written this book.

A few years ago, as I chatted with Louis Melchionne, he exclaimed to Frank Pettit and Tony Gotto, "My gosh, this fellow really knows Lionel."

Frank agreed that I knew the names of many of their fellow workers and was familiar with the standard and O gauge trains Lionel had produced.

Tony just listened. Then he said, "Roger may know Lionel. But does he really feel Lionel? Can he feel what it was like to be there?" My hope is that this book and subsequent ones will begin to answer these questions.

In 1900, Joshua Lionel Cowen founded the toy company that bore his middle name. He dominated the firm's history well into the 1950s. In one way or another, he touched all the men whose recollections fill this book.

INTRODUCTION

For me, as for most of us, the trains came first. Fascinated by the speed and color of these toys, I scarcely imagined that they had been designed and assembled by human beings. Oh, I knew they were called Lionel trains, but I had no idea why. And who could blame a six-year-old for not paying attention to who made the toys he played with? After all, I had no familiarity with the people who had produced my father's Buick or grown the carrots my mother cooked. I cared only that my trains ran whenever I wanted to enjoy them.

My concerns weren't much different when a change in careers brought me back to the world of toy trains thirty years later. I reacquainted myself with Lionel trains and reminisced about the locomotives and accessories I had once owned. Then I began learning about the models that had been made and marketed over the half-century before I received my first set in 1957. At some level, I realized that Lionel had a history, but I would have been hard-pressed to have explained that history or its significance.

Then one day, an epiphany: Watching a milk car go through its paces, I suddenly realized that someone, and a very clever someone, had devised the model I found so entertaining. Who was this person? How did he develop this landmark car? Once my mind clicked into gear, the questions never stopped: Who created all the other operating cars that so amused me? How many people worked at Lionel, producing those cars as well as miniature locomotives and accessories? How many of each item did they produce? Who hired and fired the people toiling on the assembly lines? Which models sold best? Which ones failed? Above all, why had electric trains been so popular when I was young? And why were they no longer as popular with children?

Overloaded with questions, I struggled to find answers. Unfortunately for me, the sources of information that I had learned in graduate school to consult were of minimal use. Contemporary newspapers, government files, and corporate documents either no longer existed or revealed little about Lionel. There seemed to be no way to obtain answers to the questions bombarding me. Mired in frustration, I was about to quit when I recalled a book about professional baseball that I had read years before.

In *The Glory of Their Times,* Lawrence Ritter set out to learn what baseball had meant to the men who had played the game during the first third of the twentieth century. He wanted to find out what pitching to Babe Ruth had been like, for example, and how hard it had been to hit Walter Johnson's fastball. Newspapers and documents were available, Ritter knew, but they could not tell him what he desired to know. Only the players could do that. So he spent years looking for and talking with former ballplayers.

Virtually all the greatest stars from the 1910s and 1920s had died by the time Ritter began his search in the early 1960s. Still, he managed to locate and interview dozens of elderly men who had competed against and shared locker rooms with such legendary players as Ty Cobb, Christy Mathewson, Cy Young, and Honus Wagner. By asking insightful questions and listening carefully to the tales he heard, Ritter succeeded in re-creating a golden age of American baseball that otherwise would have been lost.

"Oral history," the scholarly enterprise that *The Glory of Their Times,* among other books, had inspired, struck me as my best hope for understanding Lionel. If I could identify the salesmen, engineers, and factory supervisors and then speak with them, perhaps I could find the answers I wanted. Like Ritter, I quickly learned that the "stars"—in this case, the founders of Lionel and its top executives—were no longer alive. My disappointment was great, as I realized that the questions I wanted to ask Joshua Lionel Cowen, Mario Caruso, Lawrence Cowen, Arthur Raphael, and Joseph Bonanno would go unanswered. The temptation to quit surfaced again.

At that moment, a sympathetic editor rescued me. Dick Christianson at *Classic Toy Trains* magazine encouraged me to keep hunting for other surviving Lionel employees. Even if the giants had passed away, he reminded me, some of the men and women who had known and worked with them must be alive. Over the last six years, I have followed Dick's advice and located dozens of former Lionelers. They have led me to others, relatives and longtime friends who had helped design, produce, and test standard and O gauge trains at the company's factory in Hillside, New Jersey. Sometimes the individuals I interviewed had held positions in sales or advertising at the corporate headquarters in New York. All had memories to share and were eager to cooperate with someone still interested in what they had to say.

The result has been a number of transcribed interviews and biographical profiles published in *Classic Toy Trains*. These articles have revealed much about how Lionel was managed and how its electric trains were developed and marketed. As important, the subjects of these articles have provided photographs of executives and supervisors, company functions, and dealer displays and layouts. Thanks to their generosity, readers have become familiar with aspects of Lionel's history that had been forgotten.

Publishing the accounts and pictures of the men and women I've interviewed proved to be extremely rewarding, for both what it revealed about Lionel and how it paid tribute to individuals whose accomplishments might have been overlooked. With so many others to celebrate, I believed that the time was ripe to compile a book of these reminiscences, an "insider's history of Lionel." Most of the people I've interviewed worked there after the Second World War, an era when Lionel first dominated the toy business and then suffered devastating setbacks. Consequently, the postwar years receive an indepth treatment here, although the two decades before the war haven't been neglected. A few individuals were hired in the 1930s or even earlier, and they share valuable information about Lionel's formative years.

Most striking is the diversity of the perspectives offered by these nine former Lionel employees. Tom Pagano and Lawrence Parker share information about how toy train technology and Lionel's business practices advanced during the prewar period, when they worked closely with Mario Caruso, who oversaw production at Lionel's factory. Louis Melchionne and John DiGirolamo arrived during the Second World War, a time when production of military instruments and weapons replaced the manufacture of toy trains. Meanwhile, as Parker explains, Lionel struggled to maintain a presence in the toy field with a unique venture that he, under Caruso's guidance, sought to launch.

Jack Kindler and Jerry Lamb joined the sales force immediately after the war and grew close to the elder and younger Cowens as well as to Arthur Raphael, the firm's national sales manager. They provide anecdotes and memories about selling electric trains in the late 1940s and early 1950s, when no other toy meant so much to American boys and their families. Kindler, in particular, has much to say about how Lionel marketed its products. So does Bill Vollheim, who recalls Cowen and Joe Hanson (the advertising director) and the methods they used to convey the fun of playing with Lionel trains.

While Lamb and Kindler concentrate on the company's showroom and its display layouts, others focus on the Engineering Department housed at Lionel's plant. There, DiGirolamo labored on the electrical components of various locomotives and accessories, including many of the transformers needed to power Lionel's trains. Anthony Gotto emphasizes the contributions of a close-knit group of highly skilled model makers. Without the preliminary pieces he and his peers created, mass production would not have been possible.

Underlying the recollections of all these men is the demise of Lionel, the roots of which can be traced as far back as 1952, when Raphael died, or even 1944, when Caruso left. Almost all the subjects of this book lived through the declining years and remember the sadness and anger they felt when the Cowens surrendered control and the market for toy trains dried up. Some of them, notably George Vitt and John DiGirolamo, directed their energies toward the development and production of other kinds of items, since plans for diversifying the line were never abandoned. They devoted themselves to Lionel and hoped that they could reverse its ill fortune.

By 1969, when General Mills purchased the Lionel train line, all of these individuals had left Lionel. Their new jobs, while not always as enjoyable as what they had done at Lionel, proved to be as rewarding. In adjusting to massive changes in their lives and revealing the depth of character needed to thrive in difficult times, these men proved to be inspirations to their families and friends. Their experiences and attitudes have much to teach all of us who love the electric trains they designed, built, or sold.

Yes, the trains came first for me, and I've never lost my enthusiasm for them. Now, however, when I admire an F3 or a searchlight car or an illuminated passenger station, I think of the individuals I've met who contributed to the success of those items. All of these people, not to mention the hundreds who worked alongside them and the legendary executives at the top, deserve credit for making The Lionel Corporation the world's greatest toy train maker. They built it and, through their memories, have kept its heritage alive. Responsibility for maintaining that legacy now passes to those of us who continue to cherish the products these people made.

Tom Pagano takes time to reminisce about the many ways his family contributed to Lionel's greatness.

TOM PAGANO

Attention to the details that made Lionel great

The men who ran Lionel's factory placed great trust in their assistants and supervisors. They had to. Mario Caruso and Charles Giaimo, who served as works manager for many years before and after the Second World War, could not do everything themselves. And so, from general foremen such as Tom Caprio and Angelo Festa, they expected hard, disciplined labor. From Gus Ferri in the Model Shop and Quentin Gualtier in Tool Design, they counted on jobs performed efficiently and economically.

The Paganos provided something else. Jack and his son, Thomas, stood out for being able to keep their eyes on both the forest and the trees. They cared about the well-being of the company and gave it exceptional loyalty. The two men, one or both of whose names appeared on the payroll from 1915 to 1959, watched over the line and studied the ways various items were made. Simultaneously, they focused on the details, the innumerable little things that, when done correctly, can save thousands of dollars.

What also distinguished the Paganos was a streak of independence. Loyalty to the firm didn't mean ignoring mistakes or withholding criticism.

Jack never feared pointing out problems to the powerful Caruso, even if doing so jeopardized his job. Tom carried on that tradition. "Above all, attention to detail: that became my motto," he states. "If I believed that a procedure could be done in a better way, I wouldn't hesitate to tell my superiors." The Paganos' determination to get everything right without compromising personal ideals helped Lionel produce electric trains that were unmatched in quality.

A NEW LAND AND A NEW JOB

Sixteen-year-old Jack Pagano arrived in America in 1904. He made his way to New Haven, Connecticut, where an uncle lived, and found work in tailor shops that catered to students at nearby Yale University. After three years, by working long hours and living frugally, Jack had saved enough money to return to Italy to see his family and help two of his brothers come back to America with him.

Stitching up suits didn't consume all of Jack's hours. He found time to socialize with other fellows his age. Bicycling became his passion, and he joined a local club of enthusiasts. One of the friends he rode with was Joseph Caruso, who introduced his sister, Sarina, to Jack in 1910. A year later, Jack and Sarina married.

Among those sharing wine and cake with the bride and groom was another of Sarina's brothers, Mario. A serious man, he supervised operations at the

As a boy, Tom (front right) spent a lot of time at Lionel's factory with his father (rear left), who was a foreman when this picture was taken in 1923.

small plant where she worked. It housed the Lionel Manufacturing Company. "We make toy trains," Sarina surely had told Jack, likely adding that if he wanted a job there she would approach Mario on his behalf. Her husband listened as Mario described the company's steady growth. For the moment, however, sewing men's clothing satisfied Jack.

Life changed for the Carusos and Paganos in 1914. Lionel pulled up stakes and moved production to Newark. The tide of Italian immigrants pouring into New York City was spilling over into northern New Jersey. Mario, aware of what was happening, persuaded J. L. Cowen to take advantage of the expanding pool of men desperate for jobs. His countrymen would provide dedicated work while accepting with little question the demands made on them. Caruso's views influenced his siblings and their spouses. Sarina and her family headed south from New Haven in 1915. Casting his thread and needles aside, Jack signed on at Lionel.

Caruso paid close attention to the man who had wed his sister. Did he work hard and devote himself to his labor? Could he be trusted by the men who toiled alongside him? Did he continue to think about his job after the whistle blew at the end of the day? In every respect, Jack met the expectations his brother-in-law set forth. His work habits were exemplary, and he went out of his way to make sure materials weren't wasted as he assembled trains. Pleased by Jack's efforts, Caruso promoted him to foreman of the Car Assembly Department in 1918, a time when he needed more than ever to be able to rely on his subordinates. Lionel had

Pausing from work in the late 1930s, Tom wears a white smock much as his uncle, Mario Caruso, did.

outgrown its factory on Ogden Street in Newark, and Caruso was overseeing construction of a new facility on 21st Street in Irvington. He increasingly depended on Jack and other foremen to handle the day-to-day responsibilities.

AUTONOMY AT THE FACTORY

Caruso's esteem for Sarina's husband grew in the coming years. In February of 1925 he wrote Jack a letter, noting that he had told others at Lionel about "the splendid work you are doing, and how much of a pleasure it is to work with you." Such praise must have caused Jack's chest to swell with pride. He had proved to his stern brother-in-law that he had deserved to marry into the family. More important, he had proved to himself that he could achieve the good life that America offered.

About the same time, Caruso recommended that the Car Assembly Department, like a few others at the plant, be reorganized as a partially autonomous entity. To be specific, Lionel would order the rolling stock it needed from Jack, who would hire workers to build enough cars using machinery and

11

Jack Pagano continued to work at Lionel until his death in 1949.

materials the company supplied. As orders were filled, he would deliver the finished products to the Shipping Department, which would buy them at prices set by management. Jack would use that money to pay his employees according to piece-work rates he established. This unique arrangement would cut expenses for Lionel while giving one of its top foremen an opportunity to gain managerial experience and financial rewards.

Jack jumped at the chance. Assembly of freight and passenger cars became more efficient, even as orders swelled. The thirty or so men and women employed by Jack performed effectively, especially with the fair rates he set. Workers elsewhere in the factory watched enviously and begged for consideration when there were openings in the Car Assembly Department.

Problems arose, however, over how piece-work rates should be set. Jack believed that once a rate was set, it should not be lowered, no matter how much an employee earned, unless improved work fixtures and tools or component modifications measurably increased efficiency. Then a new rate could be established. An impatient Caruso insisted that rates be cut whenever a person earned more than 30 percent above his or her hourly wage. That way, Lionel could reduce the prices at which it purchased finished cars. Jack balked at this scheme. Sympathy and respect for the people he had hired led him to maintain the current rates. Furious at being challenged, Caruso countered in 1928 by terminating the firm's special arrangement with Jack.

The next year Caruso told Jack to take over as foreman of the Outfit Packing Department. When orders declined as the Depression worsened in 1930, Jack lost his position and was transferred to the newly organized Service Department. There he used his ample mechanical skills to repair locomotives. To his credit, Jack never allowed his spirit to flag. For example, in 1937 he marched alongside the workers picketing the factory in hopes of winning higher wages and better conditions. Through much of the Second World War and later until his death in November of 1949, Jack stayed at Lionel. Yet in key respects for this gentleman, 1928 marked the end of the good times.

BRINGING IN NEW BLOOD

Ironically, the early 1930s, when Jack's prospects looked bleak, represented a hopeful time for others in the Pagano family. Members of the next generation came of age and joined the work force. Mary, the eldest daughter, learned about the factory serving as Uncle Mario's secretary. Later, after she left to marry Frank Pettit, Lionel's development engineer, her younger sister, Anna, replaced her. Still, neither woman affected production as did their thin, quiet brother, Tom. He was to become the expert on how to make better electric trains by employing systems of controlled processes, costs, and quality in their manufacture.

"When did I start working at Lionel? Well," Tom laughs, "when I was six years old I used to accompany my father as he made his rounds as watchman on Sundays. That started in 1918. While he made his rounds, I ran trains on the test layouts or built models of airplanes and ships in the carpentry shop. Between rounds, my father helped me improve my reading. We read newspapers, magazines, and, of course, the latest Lionel catalogs."

As a teenager in the 1920s, Tom spent each summer working in the plant on 21st Street. The first year he had the unpleasant task of painting the round stop signs on no. 77 Automatic Crossing Gates. After a long day's production and cleaning the printing press, he was covered with red ink. In the years that followed Tom was given more interesting and less messy jobs that involved assembling and wiring components for various locomotives.

After graduating from high school in 1931, Tom discovered the rewards of working at Lionel. Caruso, aware that his nephew had studied mechanical drawing, assigned him to a special machine shop located across from the main plant on 21st Street. Tom worked under the supervision of John Kohke, an experienced, highly competent German toolmaker. They had to build a machine that could automatically insert and crimp a connecting pin to each rail of track after it had passed through all the roll-forming operations of the rail machine. Tom found the work fascinating and, before heading off to college in the fall, executed drawings of all pertinent parts and assemblies so that six machines could be built with interchangeable parts. "Uncle Mario walked by one day, pushed his glasses onto his forehead, and stared at my drawings." Tom says. "Then he smiled and muttered, 'Good, good.' I knew he was pleased because my next pay envelope contained a raise from 25 to 28 cents an hour."

Any questions about what to do with his life vanished. Highly motivated, Tom spent four years studying machine design and other fundamental disciplines of engineering at Stevens Institute of Technology. He returned to Lionel in 1935, hopeful of being hired and allowed to collaborate with another Stevens graduate, Joseph Bonanno, the chief engineer. But Uncle Mario had other thoughts. To broaden Tom's understanding of toy train electronics, Caruso and Charles Giaimo (assistant superintendent of manufacturing) assigned him to the Coil Winding Department. Designated assistant foreman, Tom worked under the keen eyes of Theodore Flagg, himself fairly new to Lionel. Besides gaining valuable experience, Tom again demonstrated to Caruso an eagerness to master new fields.

MOVE TOWARD SELF-SUFFICIENCY

The decision to hire Flagg represented a trend that changed the character of Lionel during the 1930s. Under the leadership of Caruso and Bonanno, the firm was striving to become virtually self-sufficient. That is, the two men overseeing production and design wanted to lower costs and increase profits by depending less on outside vendors to carry out various steps in the manufacturing and assembly processes. They promoted vertical integration—once raw materials had been procured, Lionel took all the steps necessary to transform the steel, aluminum, zinc, and plastics it purchased into finished items ready to be shipped to distributors.

To illustrate how circumstances were changing, Tom points out that in the 1920s and into the '30s, Lionel bought many electrical components from local entrepreneurs. "I'd visit the plant as a boy and watch as the armatures used on locomotives and the secondary windings for transformers were wound." Key pieces, such as the windings used for transformer primaries and for solenoids, arrived by truck, often from the Fada Radio Company on Long Island, the firm where Ted Flagg worked. Bonanno brought him to Lionel as part of a plan to lessen the company's dependence on other manufacturers. Under Flagg's guidance, the Coil Winding Department took on more complicated and costly tasks until employees excelled at them.

Caruso wanted to launch a grander scheme, and Tom was going to play a crucial role. Immediately after the First World War, Caruso and Cowen had recognized that, with German toy train makers effectively barred from the American market, the battle for supremacy would be fought by Lionel and its chief domestic rival, the Ives Manufacturing Co. Victory would go to the firm that produced smooth-running and handsome models and marketed them widely at the lowest prices. Reducing the costs of tooling without sacrificing quality was, Lionel's leaders had understood, essential to achieving their ambitious goal.

A determined Caruso had set out to persuade his partner to have all of Lionel's major tooling designed and made in his native land. He believed that as Italy struggled to rebuild its economy after the war, growth would derive, not from exporting raw materials, but from tapping the talents of men leaving the military. Brilliant designers and skilled toolmakers needed jobs; if facilities were built and customers recruited, these bright men could supply them with the tools they needed to manufacture an array of goods.

With this in mind, Caruso, given financial backing by Cowen, established Societa Meccanica La Precisa in Naples. He traveled to Italy each year, starting in 1924, to oversee the design and production of whatever tooling Lionel needed for upcoming standard and O gauge locomotives, rolling stock, and accessories. During the months he spent overseas, Caruso made certain that, in Pagano's words, "tools were designed in minute detail, both the assembly of the tool and each component part, right down to the last, small dimension." As a result, La Precisa turned out tooling that surpassed in quality and cost less than anything made by Lionel's rivals, all the while training and upgrading its labor force.

14

Tom listens as friends raise their glasses at a bachelor party held in his honor in 1942. Seated to his immediate left is Philip Marfuggi (Lionel's personnel director), followed by Charles Giaimo and Joseph Bonanno.

Caruso would have continued to rely on La Precisa except for one problem. By 1935, when Tom was hired, the situation in Europe had become precarious. The works manager followed developments in Italy and watched with mixed emotions as Benito Mussolini claimed more power for his Fascist movement. War was not out of the question, Caruso feared; neither was a government seizure of La Precisa. So he began laying the groundwork for transferring the design and production of tooling to Irvington. For Caruso, Giaimo, and Bonanno, doing so was a prudent step that would advance the firm's move toward self-sufficiency and avoid the dangers of contracting for work overseas and transporting it across the Atlantic Ocean.

TOM'S BIGGEST CHALLENGE

Lionel had employed toolmakers since its earliest years to make an assortment of small items, notably assembly fixtures and coil winding machines. Following tradition, these craftsmen designed individual tools and then constructed them from start to finish. They also maintained and repaired the large tools that were ordered from domestic vendors until La Precisa was formed to handle all major projects. "All the work that our toolmakers did was carried out in an area we called the Tool Room," Tom explains. "It was under the supervision of a foreman who acted as a master mechanic. In addition, every item, no matter what its size, was carefully labeled with the part number it produced and stored with a control card locating system in the Tool Vault, which was closely guarded by an attendant."

Sometime in 1936, Caruso expected Lionel to take the next step and begin

15

designing all its own tooling, much of which he hoped to produce within the factory. Such a task was huge, but he doubted that it could be postponed much longer. After conferring with Giaimo, he summoned Tom and gave him responsibility for developing a tool design department. Tom replied that he did not know anything about tools and dies. His uncle ignored the protests and insisted the young man prove what he had learned in college. Caruso's sole concession was to offer Tom the services of Frank Martin, a bright toolmaker. Then he made sure they had access to files from La Precisa.

From examining those documents, Tom understood that success depended on controlling the time and money spent on tool design and production. Meeting that goal required a threefold approach. First, Tom established guidelines for the design of all tools. He wanted standard sizes, so that all dies, for example, might fit on the power presses without having to be adjusted. Too often, even with tooling produced at La Precisa, items ended up damaged because setup workers had to insert shims if they hoped to fit them on the machines. Such improvisation put tooling under severe strain. If it broke, production was delayed and resources had to be diverted to fix it.

To determine a range of sizes, Tom and Frank walked down to the Tool Vault and measured the tools already in storage. Before long, they noticed that most items fell within regular categories. Once they had classified existing tools, it seemed logical to demand that all new designs adhere to standards they defined. This step, so simple and obvious to Tom, promised greater accuracy and improved safety. It would ensure that tools and machines lasted longer and produced more precise components.

Establishing design standards was only the initial step. Talented individuals able to follow those guidelines were as essential. Consequently, Tom's second move, taken simultaneously with the first, was to recruit skilled designers of the machine tools Lionel needed. With Martin's help, he posted notices throughout the plant and devised a simple test to evaluate how much applicants knew about mechanical drawing. Tom emphasized that potential tool designers must have graduated from high school. He identified some outstanding men, including Quentin Gualtier, Walter Camuso, and Bernard Perotty, all of whom became the nucleus of the staff that was working under Martin by 1938. Meanwhile, Caruso and Giaimo were overseeing construction of a modern and expanded Tool Room, in which tool designers and toolmakers would coordinate their efforts. By 1939, it was ready to open.

The third factor in achieving the firm's goal was to increase the productivity of the Tool Room. Again, Tom adopted a multidirectional approach. His plan was, first, to have the first-class skilled toolmakers do the final fitting and assembling of tools using parts prepared by less skilled people. Caruso had instituted such a system at La Precisa with success. The key was finding enterprising men willing to take on these preliminary tasks.

Fortunately, as principal aide to Giaimo, Tom had free run of the factory. He pulled aside employees who expressed an eagerness to learn how to read drawings and prepare the pieces of raw steel used for components. These men planed and shaped, milled and ground, drilled and bored each piece until it was ready to be handed to the highly skilled toolmakers.

Tom presents a safety award to members of the Heat-Treating Department.

Productivity was improved in a second, indirect manner, as Caruso and Giaimo recognized that some designs were too expensive and time-consuming to be done in-house. They developed a network of tool and die manufacturers in New York and New Jersey to which they channeled projects. The best example, according to Tom, was Scandia Machine & Die Corp., a Brooklyn firm that made the major tools used on the 700E and 763 Hudsons. Dollin Corp. and Gebauer Die & Tool Co., both located near the plant, produced a number of molds that Lionel or vendors under contract used for die-casting projects. Their contributions were vital because the need to introduce new products every year had taxed Lionel's own toolmaking capabilities to their maximum.

The third way Tom upgraded the Tool Room might have been the most advantageous in the long run. He inaugurated a program to train more toolmakers. Young men were invited to participate in an apprentice program. They were recruited from production departments based on their past performance and recommendations from their supervisors.

Tom established a schedule whereby each trainee was required to perform a given number of hours per year on each machine tool in the Tool Room and Machine Shop. In addition, tool layout and precision measuring methods, along with important manual functions, were covered, all under the supervision of the Tool Room and Machine Shop foremen and key first-class workers. A system of periodic grading was created to monitor progress.

This work was done every day. Twice each week, however, the trainees spent the afternoon studying tool design, drafting, and mathematics with instructors from the county vocational school. More prestigious, higher-paying positions awaited them at Lionel when they graduated after four years. "The program worked beautifully for everyone," Tom states. "The men enrolled in it benefited by improving their skills, and over the years, Lionel built up a group of almost eighty people with unique skills in such mechanical arts as toolmaking, precision machining, instrument assembly, and quality control." The firm would need every one of them during the Second World War to help fulfill all the military contracts it was awarded.

"In the ensuing years," Tom adds, "my greatest satisfaction has come from learning of the successful impact these people have made after leaving Lionel. Some founded their own toolmaking and manufacturing companies. Others went on to fill important positions in manufacturing management with notable firms, and still others I hired to fill demanding niches in my new associations. I was familiar with their skills and trusted their work."

TIME TO SETTLE DOWN

By the time the war interrupted toy train production, Tom was more than ready to catch his breath. He had accomplished so much in his first seven years at Lionel, only occasionally failing to satisfy his demanding uncle. Above all, he had almost single-handedly built up the Tool Design Department, which, by 1942, had become a hive of activity. Over the next three years, designers tackled an array of projects submitted by the nation's armed forces. Tom watched proudly as the staff turned out plans for the tooling to make various precision instruments. He watched from afar, however, as Caruso had not asked him to run the department when Frank Martin left. Instead, the works manager hired an outsider, Joseph DeVito, whose administrative abilities nicely matched his mechanical skills.

For the truth was, Tom was too good to be kept in a single department. When Giaimo had been stricken with multiple sclerosis in 1937 and taken an indefinite leave from the plant, Tom had assumed many of his responsibilities as assistant superintendent. Once more, he had proved himself in the eyes of Uncle Mario. After Giaimo returned and was promoted to superintendent, Caruso named his nephew an assistant superintendent, with responsibility for several important departments. For someone barely thirty years old, exercising so much authority was a tremendous accomplishment.

Settling into the routines of his job made life easier for Tom. That was fortunate because he had married, and his wife and he were looking forward to starting a family. Louise was all too familiar with Lionel, having worked as a nurse in its clinic prior to the war. She was glad that Tom's position kept him from being drafted, although Lionel's defense projects compelled him to spend long hours at the factory. Often he didn't come home until late at night. He worked a ten-hour day, ate a quick supper at the plant, and then met with all the key department heads to prepare quotations for new projects.

Perhaps surprisingly, not much changed for Tom when Caruso stunned everyone by leaving Lionel in October of 1944. Feeling stifled there, Caruso wanted to pursue other business opportunities. Before resigning, he dangled jobs in front of a handful of employees he hoped would also leave. Tom was not among them. Who would take over as works manager remained uncertain for more than two years, with some insiders predicting that Bonanno would claim the job. Instead, despite the lingering effects of his physical disability, Giaimo was selected in 1947. He knew Tom's capability and soon broadened the latter's responsibilities as assistant superintendent of all parts production so that position also included plant engineering and maintenance functions.

Tom's job required nothing less than ensuring that the plant's manufacturing capacity could handle the growing demands for Lionel trains.

Consequently, he had to plan for and construct more floor space, design and install efficient infrastructure equipment (power and lighting, compressed air, and steam and water distribution systems), and project ongoing requirements for production machinery. Without skipping a beat, Tom was expected to take whatever steps were necessary to establish a methods department. There, manufacturing engineers under the direction of Walter Camuso used design details and samples to process the most efficient ways by which to mass-produce the components and subassemblies of specific items and to plan their final assembly.

Sometime in the early 1950s, Tom posed holding one of Lionel's new locomotives.

As should be clear, Tom somehow touched every type of train and accessory Lionel made from the late 1940s through the 1950s. His influence began when, with other members of the Planning Board, he discussed the details, analyzed the costs, and coordinated production of approved additions to the line. The initial manufacturing steps, highlighted by the design and construction of new tooling, fell under Giaimo's jurisdiction as superintendent. Then came the procurement of raw materials and the planning and scheduling of production, areas handled by departments reporting to John Giampolo, the other assistant superintendent, who was in charge of production control.

The departments under Tom then took over, manufacturing and finishing all the required components. He supervised the departments in which parts were prepared for the different subassemblies: molding and casting, stamping, machining, welding and soldering, plating, powdered metallurgy, and painting. Tom consulted the foremen regularly to ensure that everything was proceeding on schedule, all produced under controlled conditions of quality and cost. Every part not acquired from an outside vendor demanded his attention. It wasn't simple work, because, as an article in *All Aboard at Lionel,* the employee newsletter, stated: "There can be no slips anywhere along the line for, in management circles, there is no allowance for 'scrap' and no market for alibis."

Although the Tool Design Department wasn't considered part of Tom's bailiwick, he maintained interest in what happened there. He conferred often with his old friend Quentin Gualtier, whom Tom had persuaded to return to Lionel after the war to head that department. Tom's ideas for improved pro-

A happy moment for Lionel's brain trust in the mid-1950s. Seated (left to right): Ed Zier (comptroller), Joseph Bonanno, J. L. Cowen, Charles Giaimo, and John Giampolo. Standing (left to right): Tom Pagano, Philip Marfuggi, Lawrence Cowen, Alan Ginsburg (executive vice-president), Sam Belser (national sales manager), and Frank Pettit.

duction machinery and more efficient retooling of key components helped Quentin design them for construction. Tom also assisted in a reorganization of the Tool Room that encouraged toolmakers to specialize in certain types of components as a way of further cutting costs and increasing the precision of their work. No wonder his peers lauded him as one of the few people at Lionel who was truly "indispensable."

LIVING PROOF

Tom proved to be indispensable for a reason other than his attention to detail. Lionel's executives praised him as proof of how far someone could progress through hard work and loyalty. A profile published in the October 1948 issue of *All Aboard at Lionel* emphasized that he always looked for problems to be solved and sought to better himself through independent study. Even after Tom finished his undergraduate education, he pushed himself to enroll in night courses in metallurgy and industrial engineering. Sure, Tom's two sons and hobbies kept him busy. "But his main interests in life are his work and his studies." In fact, the author concluded by describing Tom as "One of the most active individuals in the plant . . . virtually everywhere at once [because] his advice is constantly being sought."

The point was clear: Other employees should follow Tom's example if they hoped to get ahead. Admittedly, he couldn't boast of many singular achievements, such as inventing the remote-control whistle installed in Lionel's steam engines as Giaimo had done or developing new accessories the way his brother-in-law, Frank Pettit, did. All the same, Tom had achieved something as notable. He had become the exemplary Lionel worker and so deserved to feel secure at the firm.

As important as his solid work habits, Tom never forgot the need to help others. This was true at the factory, the profile in *All Aboard at Lionel* pointed out, where "his amiable disposition has made him extremely popular." If anything, Tom's fierce desire to improve himself convinced him of the wisdom of assisting others. Rather than wait for other men to lift themselves up to his level of expertise, Tom offered a helping hand, just as long as the beneficiaries of his aid showed initiative and loyalty. As

While serving on the city council in Madison, New Jersey, Tom presented Mayor Tom Taber, an avid Lionel collector and railroad historian, with a special display of a no. 2321 Lackawanna Train Master. In 1959, he arranged for President Dwight Eisenhower to receive a unique display of a no. 1862 General steam engine.

proof, one need only look at the training programs he launched before and after the war at Lionel as well as Tom's involvement in civic affairs.

Sadly, Tom's dedication to the company and disdain for those who sought only to augment their power there couldn't ensure his survival. In October of 1959, the Cowen family sold its controlling interest to a group headed by Roy Cohn, a distant relative notorious for assisting Senator Joseph McCarthy in a search for subversion in the Army. Cohn, disturbed by Lionel's declining profits and eager to assert his authority, decided to clean house at the plant. Among the first to be discharged in 1959 was Charles Giaimo. Tom, identified so closely with the works manager, also was asked to resign. He did so with regret, yet felt confident that he would land on his feet and find employment where his abilities were recognized.

Tom did exactly that, despite being nearly fifty years old when he left Lionel. Eventually he secured the position of manufacturing consultant at the Atlas Sound Division of American Trading and Production Corporation. He helped the division grow and was asked to manage a three-plant operation that built commercial loudspeakers in three states. Tom enjoyed a rewarding career there that lasted until he finally retired at age eighty. Success, he believes, was simply a matter of working in a firm that appreciated his experience, imagination, loyalty, and industry. His contributions to Lionel's growth reflected those traits and the ability of Caruso and Giaimo to put them to good use. They realized that Tom was the prototype of the ideal Lionel employee and linked the company's destiny to his.

Lawrence Parker recalled his years at Lionel with affection. The people and products left memories that lasted until he died in November of 1996.

LAWRENCE PARKER
A Yankee Comes to Lionel

The popular view of Lionel's factory is that it was dominated by Italians. There's a fair amount of truth to this generalization. Mario Caruso and Charles Giaimo, who held the prestigious position of works manager, had come from Italy. They were assisted by men with obvious Italian surnames, such as Joseph and William Bonanno, Philip and Rex Marfuggi, John Giampolo, Tom Pagano, and Anthony LaFauci. A list of foremen from the 1920s on would have revealed others who took pride in their Italian heritage.

Of course, individuals of other ethnic backgrounds worked on assembly lines during the prewar and postwar eras. Aware of the prevailing view even then, executives rarely hesitated to point out the Germans and Irish who had risen to positions of responsibility. They emphasized that Lionel was, as America itself sought to be, a melting pot in which men and women from different traditions labored together to build the trains prized by all kids.

Still, the atmosphere at the Lionel factory, especially in the 1930s when Caruso managed it with an iron hand, was distinctly Italian. There were a handful of exceptions, however, and one outsider who earned Caruso's trust boasted a background strikingly different from his. Lawrence Parker was a true Yankee, a New Englander who could trace his roots back to the *Mayflower*. He arrived at Lionel as a young man and gained the confidence of Caruso. In time, Parker followed his mentor to New England, where, during the Second World War, they made wood toys and assessed Lionel's future.

A FRIENDLY TIP LEADS TO LIONEL

If things had gone as Larry Parker had planned, he never would have ended up at Lionel. Instead, he would have been posted to an embassy in Europe or some more exotic locale. For his dream was a career in America's foreign service. That dream led Parker first to Bates College in his home state of Maine and then, after graduation in 1932, to the distinguished Fletcher School of Law and Diplomacy, just outside Boston. His sharp mind and pleasing personality seemed to ensure success in the field of his choice.

But conditions were difficult for anyone graduating from college during the Great Depression. Parker's job search proved more frustrating than he had imagined. Month after month passed following his graduation in 1935 and no offers came forth. Then a friend who had recently returned from Europe mentioned that on the voyage he had met Mario Caruso. "Perhaps," the friend suggested, "Mr. Caruso has an opening for you." Parker sent a letter to Lionel.

Caruso replied with an invitation to visit the plant. In the meantime, Parker received offers from Abraham & Strauss and Chase National Bank in New York. He had tentatively accepted the first job, but decided there was no harm in traveling to Lionel. Once he arrived, Caruso gave him a tour. Parker, who had worked as an apprentice industrial engineer at a woolen mill in the year after finishing his bachelor's degree, knew enough about manufacturing to be impressed by what he saw at Lionel. The machinery was up-to-date and well tended, and the laborers displayed high levels of discipline and efficiency. He forgot Abraham & Strauss and turned his attention to Lionel.

THE OUTSIDER MOVES IN

In an almost nonchalant fashion, Caruso offered to make the 25-year-old applicant his administrative assistant. Parker accepted and was told to report to the factory on January 2, 1936. During the intervening weeks, he was asked to stop by Lionel's showroom. There he met J. L. Cowen, who instructed Arthur Raphael and his sales staff to familiarize the newcomer with the mechanics of various electric trains and accessories. They did so until Raphael dispatched Parker to L. Bamberger & Co., a department store in Newark, to help demonstrate trains during the holiday season.

Before Parker knew it, Christmas had passed and he was settling into a small office at the factory, right next door to Caruso. To make sure everyone at the plant understood that the young man should not be ignored or taken advantage of, Caruso instructed the maintenance crew to letter his door, "Mr. Parker." Now, however, it was up to Larry to maintain his superior's trust.

Initially, that meant handling the mundane responsibilities of an administrative assistant. "My job," Parker explained, "was to take notes on the engineering and manufacturing decisions. Then I had to follow up to make sure they were carried out." This second part of his job proved challenging but enjoyable. Parker became friendly with Joseph Bonanno, the chief engineer, and Charles Giaimo, the assistant superintendent in charge of manufacturing. "Charlie was a great guy, thoroughly nice and very able."

Parker worked successfully with Bonanno and Giaimo, presumably because they realized that Larry posed no threat. The young man might have Caruso's ear, but he didn't crave power. Maybe that's why William Lawson, one of the few non-Italians in a high position at the plant, told Parker "he had never seen an outsider like him penetrate the upper circle of management."

What Caruso initially thought of his new employee can only be imagined. Approaching fifty, the works manager acted and looked older than his years. Hard work, innovative tinkering, and loyalty to the company had enabled him to rise rapidly at Lionel until he was second in command to Cowen. While the latter supervised the corporate office, "M. C.," as he was known, ruled the factory. He commanded the respect of every worker and expected deferential treatment from supervisors and assembly hands alike.

Caruso couldn't help but be aware of how different Parker was from virtually everyone else in authority at Lionel. The young man not only had gone to college, he had earned an advanced degree. Moreover, his family had long been settled in the United States, unlike many of the workers at Lionel, including Caruso, who had been born in Italy and remained tied culturally and socially to the old country. Parker knew how to dress with style. He felt comfortable with people who were richer or smarter than he. And he never doubted that eventually he would move up in the business world.

At the same time, Caruso must have been aware that Parker shared key traits with him. Both men believed strongly in the importance of hard work on the part of a labor force that should arrive on time and put in an honest day's work. They believed in investing in the best machines and updating production techniques constantly in order to manufacture outstanding, reliable goods in the most efficient and economical manner.

Further, Larry's loyalty differed from that of the many others at the factory who were related to Caruso or had married one of his sisters. He did owe his job to the works manager, but an advanced education and lack of familial ties meant Parker could move elsewhere should the job at Lionel not prove satisfactory. Caruso could not, therefore, take his assistant for granted. Rather, he would become increasingly dependent on Parker. Their relationship, as a result, grew more complicated over the next decade.

TESTED BY A STRIKE

The first real test of Parker's competence and the extent to which Caruso could rely on him came in 1937, slightly more than a year after he joined

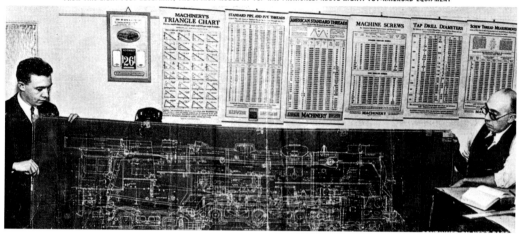

When Life Magazine came calling in 1937, Larry (left) helped show off plans for the no. 700E Hudson that Lionel was about to unveil.

Lionel. As typically happened after the rush for trains in November and December, approximately half the work force was furloughed after New Year's. From more than 1,100 workers, the payroll of the plant was reduced by 50 percent. Among the 550 or so laborers left were many skilled toolmakers and machinists who were disgusted by the low wages they earned. The time had come, they decided, to take a stand and challenge Caruso's control.

Nearly 300 hands approached the Newark lodge of the International Association of Machinists about representing them in negotiations with Lionel. According to the *Newark Evening News* of February 16, 1937, they demanded recognition of their right to unionize as well as a minimum increase in their hourly pay from 25 to 40 cents. The disgruntled laborers also called for "proper ventilation, sanitation and safeguards on machines." Unless Caruso acceded to their requests, they vowed to go on strike.

Lionel's works manager, like manufacturers and superintendents throughout the Northeast and Midwest at the time, opposed any movement that aimed to limit his power. He believed that workers ought to be happy to have a job when economic conditions were uncertain and consumer demands were sluggish. Having scant sympathy for the workers' position, he refused to meet with them. The gauntlet was thrown down; a strike was called.

Picket lines were set up outside the plant. Caruso tried to ignore them and to entice anyone desperate enough for a job to come to Lionel. Before long, rumors spread of strikers being intimidated by thugs hired by the company. Local police were called to safeguard the strikers, and officials of the American Federation of Labor called on city and state politicians to compel Lionel to settle the strike. Caruso, meanwhile, looked to Parker to deal with the newspapers and upstage the union. He needed his assistant's diplomatic talents to maintain his reputation and find a solution.

Perhaps prodded by Parker, Caruso offered a 15 percent raise if workers called off the strike. He promised machinists and tool makers an hourly increase of 5 cents, a dime less than they wanted. Furthermore, Lionel agreed to consider hiring back many of those who had dared walk the picket lines. With times so tough and money scarce, striking workers saw no choice but to surrender. They voted to accept Lionel's proposal and hoped they would be able to get back their old jobs. Peace returned to the plant, and Parker had acquitted himself in the eyes of his boss.

NEW PEOPLE AND NEW PROJECTS

The strike in early 1937 represented a turning point at Lionel for Mario Caruso. Never before had his power been so seriously challenged. Although he defeated the strikers and forced them to return to Lionel on terms he had dictated, he found himself exhausted by the effort. Determined not to be distracted from production again, he altered the upper management of the factory. He hired Philip Marfuggi, a law school graduate and former wrestler who had wed

Caruso's niece, to handle industrial relations and personnel matters. By relinquishing control of this vital area, Caruso indirectly conceded that times were changing and he couldn't hope to dominate his employees so completely.

Parker discovered that Marfuggi was a personable fellow, burly and sometimes overbearing yet flexible enough to compromise with labor without undermining the company's control. The two got along well, and Marfuggi learned he could trust and depend on Parker to help him in difficult situations. In 1937 they launched an employee newsletter, which Parker named *Lionel Lines*. And they arranged the outings on a cruise ship up the Hudson that were, for management and workers alike, the highlight of each summer. "That's when I learned that Cowen and Raphael were expert bridge players," Larry laughed. "They would take me for a week's salary if I wasn't careful."

Larry cherished his friendship with Mario Caruso and members of the works manager's extended family, which included Philip Marfuggi (left), who oversaw all matters of employee relations.

To earn that money, Parker kept looking for projects that would benefit Lionel. There wasn't much he could do to improve the electric train line; it was well established and beginning to prosper again, thanks in large part to the innovations credited to Joseph Bonanno. One improvement Parker made was printing illustrations of accessories on the side of boxes.

Broadening the product line opened new opportunities for Parker. Right from the start, he supported efforts to market an operating model airplane. Caruso liked this enthusiasm. After learning that Parker devoted his spare time to studying modern industrial engineering techniques, especially in the field of time and motion study, Caruso asked him to help organize the line that assembled the no. 50 Electric Airplane. As if that weren't enough, he told his administrative assistant to write an instruction sheet for the new toy.

Conversations with Caruso led to the suggestion that Lionel offer chemistry sets to compete with those of Porter Chemical and The A. C. Gilbert Co. Cowen favored the idea and insisted that Lionel do everything possible to have something on the market by the holiday season of 1941. He told William Bonanno, brother of the chief engineer and supervisor of the shipping and service departments, to acquire the chemicals, vials, test tubes, and other materials to be packaged in the sets. Parker was assigned the task of compiling an instruction manual that would outline an array of experiments junior chemists could perform with what he named Lionel Chem-Lab.

It took every bit of time Parker could find when he wasn't handling his regular responsibilities to devise experiments and procure chemicals needed for the new sets. Most difficult was writing the manual, which Parker did despite not having a degree in chemistry. Recognizing his limitations, he recommended that Lionel print it with the name of a chemistry professor as its editor. Fortunately, Lionel recognized that Parker deserved credit for the excellence of the manual, and the board of directors voted him a $400 bonus. Just as satisfying, Raphael penned a letter of congratulations to Larry for writing a manual that surpassed that of Porter and Gilbert.

UNCERTAIN TIMES FOR CARUSO

"My wife and I went on a shopping spree with the $400," Larry recalls. "And Raphael's praise meant a lot to me." But events beyond Lionel soon overshadowed whatever success Chem-Lab had brought. For the holiday season of 1941 was cast in gloom caused by the Japanese attack on Pearl Harbor. Toy trains and chemistry sets suddenly meant little in a land where sons and husbands were about to be sent overseas and the future was unsure.

Parker recognized the change immediately and wasn't surprised that Chem-Lab didn't sell well. Not long afterward, in early 1942, the Food and Drug Administration informed Lionel that it frowned on the firm's shipping chemicals across state lines. Even worse, federal restrictions on using metal for consumer goods prevented Lionel from cataloging more than a rudimentary line in 1942 and prohibited the production of electric trains in 1943 and 1944.

Subtle yet valuable contributions gained Larry respect from Cowen and Caruso. For example, he compiled the company's first employee handbook in 1938. Not long afterward, he promoted the idea of adding illustrations to the boxes used for Lionel's largest accessories.

Fortunately for Lionel, contracts to produce instruments and measuring devices for the United States Navy and Army Signal Corps more than made up for lost sales in trains. Beginning in 1940, the factory shifted from playthings to war materiel. Parker's responsibilities changed as well, and he worked with Caruso to ensure that production proceeded smoothly. The company's welfare depended on its manufacturing compasses, telegraph keys, binnacles, and other items according to the specifications of the armed forces.

All the same, the future looked uncertain to Caruso. The effort by workers to unionize, which he had defeated in 1937, could not be contained. Negotiations continued through the following years with Marfuggi, and at last in 1942 Lionel lost the battle. The United Paper, Novelty and Toyworkers Union secured the right to represent assembly-line workers. A disappointed Caruso realized he was losing control over the work force he had recruited.

Caruso also worried about his family's role at Lionel. He was nearing 60, and Cowen had already passed that milestone: Who would take over when they retired? The answer, to Caruso's dismay, was Cowen's son, Lawrence, who had joined the board of directors in 1937 and moved up to vice president three years later. Caruso never got along with the younger Cowen, who he doubted possessed the discipline and expertise to guide Lionel in the coming years. Similarly, he worried that there would be no place in the firm's upper echelon for his children, especially his son, Anthony.

Finally, Caruso couldn't help wondering what would happen to the investments he had made in Italy. His principal concern was the Societa Meccanica La Precisa, the enterprise he had established in Naples and administered since the mid-1920s to develop tooling for Lionel's electric trains. Throughout the 1920s and '30s, Caruso had invested funds from Lionel to improve the facilities at La Precisa and raise the quality of its work. In return, he had been able to reduce the costs of toolmaking for Lionel while ensuring a steady stream of beautifully designed tools and models for locomotives and accessories.

As America's relations with Italy deteriorated in the late 1930s and early '40s, the future of La Precisa became precarious. Caruso could no longer travel to Naples to oversee the firm; consequently, he relied on its toolmaking facilities less and less. Once war was declared, he feared that his investments in La Precisa and the surrounding real estate would be lost. Since Mussolini had nationalized the factory to make munitions for Italy's war effort, Caruso had reason to fear that La Precisa would be bombed.

To provide for his family's well-being today and tomorrow, Caruso began considering new business opportunities, ones he could control and bequeath to his children. Having once lived in Connecticut and being familiar with the solid work habits and streak of independence that characterized New Englanders, he looked to that region as a place to put his money.

With Lionel producing military and naval instruments, Caruso needed to find some way to capitalize on federal contracts without jeopardizing the company's prospects. Rather than divert business from Lionel, he wanted to improve upon it. The answer came to him as he realized that many of the items manufactured at Lionel had to be shipped from the factory in wooden cases purchased from outside firms. Caruso wondered if he could take this business for himself and thus legally steer money spent by Lionel to his family. He would, therefore, enter the packaging business.

BACK TO NEW ENGLAND

Once Caruso had decided what he was going to do, he had to find a place to make wood containers of varying sizes. Discussions with Parker about the people, economy, and resources of Maine convinced Caruso to look there. He wanted an abandoned yet viable manufacturing facility located near forests that could provide the necessary lumber. It should already have a railroad spur for bringing in raw materials and shipping finished goods.

"Caruso loaned me his car do exploratory work in Maine," Parker remembered. He located two abandoned paper mills in Gardiner and an empty shoe factory in Richmond. Then the Maine Publicity Bureau told him about an abandoned woodworking plant in West Paris, a small inland community. Parker passed that tip along to Caruso, who flew to Maine in March and joined his assistant. "We checked out the West Paris and Richmond facilities," Parker notes, "and ended up buying both in April of 1944."

The factory in Richmond was larger and in better condition. Caruso, who believed fervently that Lionel should feature chemistry sets in its line, planned to use this multiple-story facility to assemble Chem-Labs. Production had been halted by wartime restrictions, but Caruso saw no reason why Lionel shouldn't resume work on chemistry outfits when peace returned.

The fifty-year-old plant in West Paris that Caruso had purchased through his daughter Rosa was another story. "It was in terrible shape," Parker pointed out. "It had no power, no plumbing, no electrical wiring. There was a large hole in the sagging roof over the mill room,

During the war, Larry helped negotiate the purchase of this factory in West Paris, Maine, where Lionel made wood containers and toys.

and snow had covered the floor." The newly appointed plant manager got to work and did his best to refurbish the aging structure over the next two months.

What were Caruso's plans? The *Lewiston Daily Sun,* in neighboring Lewiston, reported in its April 3, 1944, issue that the factory would be used for "manufacture of finished hardwood boxes for the Navy and wooden equipment for the U. S. Signal Corps." However, hints that Caruso hoped to accomplish much more emerged from a document filed there in July.

Not long before, he had created a new enterprise, called C-8 Laboratories (the "C" stood for Caruso, and the "8" referred to Caruso, his wife, and their six children, all of whom were listed as directors). According to the certificate of association for purpose of engaging in mercantile enterprise, C-8 intended to manufacture and sell a variety of wood and plastic items, including "advertising displays, . . . Junior Scientific Sets, . . . and packing devices." Caruso was planning to enter a number of fields.

HARD TIMES IN WEST PARIS

While Caruso gazed into the future, his assistant toiled to get the enterprise in West Paris off the ground. Though still on Lionel's payroll, currently as supervisor of the Printing Department, Parker would spend nearly all the next year in New England. He was first instructed to select a name for Caruso's venture. "Because West Paris was in Oxford County," he explained, "I suggested Oxford Wood and Plastics Company." Caruso liked it, particularly since he wanted to engage in plastics molding there.

Difficult and expensive as it was to refurbish the factory, Parker faced still more trying times when he sought to hire experienced woodworkers and to secure adequate lumber. Caruso kept pressing him to move ahead quickly with constructing the wood cases Lionel needed to package compasses and binna-

30

cles for the Navy and the Signal Corps. Unfortunately for Larry, the pool of able-bodied laborers wasn't large because nearly all the young men in the area were in the armed forces. Men beyond the draft age were in demand at the two other woodworking plants in town and a nearby feldspar mine.

Acquiring enough lumber also brought Parker nightmares. Much of the acreage surrounding West Paris had claims on it. Competition for the yellow birch that Parker needed was fierce, so much so that he ended up looking over the Canadian border. He had to purchase supplies from Quebec, which increased his expenses and angered Caruso. Relations between the two men continued to fray as the summer and autumn of 1944 wore on. Parker begged for more money to pay employees, improve the factory, and buy lumber. Caruso, meanwhile, complained about rising costs and low productivity.

Blind to the problems Parker was encountering, Caruso focused instead on broadening the range of products in West Paris. Toys were the obvious choice. Another of his daughters, Teresa, had already shared with her father some ideas she had for wood pull toys and a large rocker. Caruso realized that Oxford Wood and Plastics could market them through Lionel and take advantage of its vast network of distributors across the United States. He approved her designs and asked Ernesto Peruggi, an artist associated with Lionel's Engineering Department, to refine them. Peruggi did so and received nine design patents in August of 1944 for various toys.

Once Caruso elected to expand into toy production, he must have been in touch with J. L. Cowen. With Lionel forbidden to manufacture electric trains, Cowen most likely would have supported any idea that could keep the company a presence in the toy industry. He had promoted the disastrous paper train in late 1943, so he probably would not have balked at plans for a line of wood toys meant for young boys and girls.

With Lionel's top management eager to move ahead, the next task was to secure orders. Again, Parker played a key role. He asked Louis Melchionne, recently assigned the task of organizing the new Reproduction Department, to put together a four-page brochure advertising the new line, which was named Lion-Eds. Blessed with a love of pastels as well as a sense of whimsy, Louis proceeded to put together a unique brochure. On the front were two gleeful lambs; inside, he illustrated the large rocking toy that was expected to be the backbone of the line. Parker liked what he saw and recommended that a child be shown riding the toy. To help Louis add this touch, he passed along a photograph of his young daughter, Judy.

THE END OF LION-EDS

Production of the wood instrument cases and rocking toys slowly picked up in the summer and autumn of 1944. Parker, who admitted that he knew nothing about woodworking when he moved to Maine ("I didn't know a plane from a saw!"), thought he was making excellent progress. The workers, directed by Patrick Tomaro, a longtime Lionel supervisor transferred to New

Laurence C. Parker

L. C. Parker, formerly of Dept. 18
and Pat Tomaro of Dept 41 recently
left for West Paris, Maine where
they will assume new duties.
Mr. Parker and Mr. Tomaro have
been associated with The Lionel Corporation for many years; Larry was
Supervisor of the Printing Department and Pat was foreman of Department 41 and 27A.
Both men were liked very much
and we're sure their former associates
shall miss them. The Lionel employees as well as the management
hope they will be as successful in
West Paris as they were in Irvington.

*At Caruso's request, Larry left New Jersey and set-
tled in Maine to serve as manager of Oxford Wood
and Plastics Co., as he named Lionel's venture.*

England by Caruso, had improved as well. All the same, problems remained with obtaining lumber and keeping down production costs.

The rocking toy was a headache to make, Parker stated. Machines cut out the profile of each side and the seat, but decoration was time-consuming. Five separate steps were required to add the detailed screen-printing and hand-painting on a toy whose suggested retail price of $18.75 was somewhat high. Parker concluded that fewer than 500 of the Lionel Dog Rockers were made. Even so, plans were made to expand the Lion-Eds line with pull and stacking toys for toddlers. A second brochure was printed, probably in early 1945 for the upcoming American Toy Fair in New York. However, Parker doubted that the items shown were ever made, most likely because buyers for wholesale houses showed only minimal interest in them.

Instead, like most other Americans, they were looking ahead to the end of the conflict and the resumption of normal life. For Lionel, that meant returning to the production of electric trains. Wood toys no longer had much meaning to the firm's future. That fact, coupled with Caruso's resignation from Lionel in October 1944, most likely spelled the end of the Lion-Eds. Interestingly, however, Caruso continued to operate his plant in West Paris and maintained a lovely estate there through 1950. His company kept on making wood boxes and cases, some of which were surely purchased by Lionel for the chemistry and construction sets it marketed in 1946–47 and 1947–49, respectively.

TIME TO START ANEW

Larry Parker also watched as plans for the Lion-Eds line fell apart in the spring of 1945. He wondered what the future held for Oxford Wood and Plastics, especially with Caruso's complaints about expenses and productivity increasing. A tense summer gave way to an equally tense fall. Caruso announced in October that he was flying to Maine to confer with Parker about what he was doing with all the money sent by C-8. (Lionel invested nothing in Oxford Wood and Plastics, according to Parker.)

Concerned about his future, disenchanted with the tight control Caruso held over the West Paris factory, and worried that he would be fired, Parker decided to break with the man he considered a mentor. He wrote Caruso a terse letter in which he expressed a wish to explore new opportunities in industrial management. Possibly surprised that his assistant had made the first move, Caruso did nothing to change Parker's mind.

Little Judy Parker posed on one of the rocking toys produced as part of the Lion-Eds line. This picture was soon used in a brochure distributed to the toy industry to promote the line.

Caruso came to his senses in December. When the new plant manager handed in his resignation after only three weeks on the job, Caruso realized how much he needed Parker. By then it was too late. Parker, determined to remain in New England, had found a new position. His experience with Lionel made him a strong candidate for an opening at The A. C. Gilbert Co., which produced Erector and Mysto-Magic sets and two items close to Parker's heart: chemistry outfits and electric trains. Mr. Gilbert interviewed Parker and offered him a job in the Cost and Payroll Department. Larry accepted and, after being promoted to production manager, stayed for another decade.

Parker lost contact with Caruso and Cowen, though not before each tried to lure him back. J. L., discovering that Gilbert, his chief rival, was about to hire Larry, countered with the offer of a job in Lionel's advertising department in 1946. Several months later, a chastened Caruso first telegraphed and later wrote Parker, requesting that they meet to discuss "the future of Oxford and Richmond." He closed his letter of November 5, 1946, "I believe we can get together in a way satisfactory to both of us."

Having his former bosses ask him to return soothed Parker's ego, but he never seriously entertained either offer. "I had no intention to even consider returning or working for Caruso again," he declared. He is more generous with Lionel: "I appreciated Mr. Cowen's offer and knew it would be fun to work with Joe Hanson, the new advertising director. But I declined and never regretted the years I spent at Gilbert. They were exciting and gave me opportunities to expand my knowledge and apply what I had learned."

That interest in sharing what he had learned caused Parker to leave Gilbert in 1955 and accept a position at the University of New Haven. He remained in academe until retiring in the early 1970s. His keen wit and sharp mind made him a favorite of his students, just as those qualities enabled him to gain the trust of Caruso, Cowen, and Gilbert. As Parker reminisced, "I had opportunities to learn from the best men manufacturing electric trains."

Louis Melchionne sits at the drawing board where he decorated trains and illustrated instruction sheets and service manuals for Lionel.

LOUIS MELCHIONNE
The Most Interesting Job at Lionel

Everyone familiar with postwar Lionel trains knows Louis Melchionne. Not by name, because he was one of the many individuals who worked at the Lionel factory and never received adequate recognition. Louis didn't eat in the executive dining room and wasn't feted at the American Toy Fair. But as head of Lionel's Reproduction Department, he left his mark on virtually every item made between 1942 and 1967.

Have you studied the feathers that grace the nos. 3474 and 6464-100 Western Pacific boxcars? Louis designed them. Or have you admired the stripes that add elegance to the early GGls and Santa Fe F3s? Louis made them. In fact, stripes were a specialty of his; he added them to Lionel's version of the Norfolk & Western class J steam engine as well.

Louis also prepared artwork for the instruction sheets packed with every outfit and the service manuals that showed how to repair each train and accessory. He painted prototypes of rolling stock, designed billboards, printed Lionel newsletters and stationery, sketched labels for boxes, and drew flags for road racing sets. No wonder Frank Pettit, the firm's development engineer, insists that Louis had the most interesting job at the company.

ARRIVING AT LIONEL

Louis Melchionne, vibrant and funny at the age of 90, is one of those people you immediately like. Whether it's his sincerity or sense of humor, twinkling eyes or gift of gab, you find yourself drawn to him. Those characteristics, along with his deft touch and optimistic attitude, have served him well. He has survived situations that would have defeated others, including the firings that rocked Lionel after Roy Cohn took control in late 1959. Fate has smiled on Louis, and deservedly so.

Unlike many supervisors at Lionel, who found jobs there during or right after high school, Louis arrived when he was in his thirties. By then he had peddled bananas, studied anatomy and drawing, run an athletic club, loaded beer trucks, and retouched photographs for a living. The last endeavor had brought Louis into

Unlike other factory personnel, who felt only fear when dealing with Mario Caruso, Louis Melchionne remembered him with respect and warmth. In 1943, he made this sketch of the works manager, who offered "a college education during the few years I worked for him."

partnership with Cliff Rosa, an artist who enlisted in the armed services right after the United States entered the Second World War. For that reason, Louis was looking for work again as 1942 dawned.

A neighbor named Ralph Caprio, who managed the pharmacy at Lionel's factory, told Louis that the company was hiring. Louis applied for a job, interviewing with Lawrence Parker. Then he waited months for Parker to make up his mind and send an offer. At last, an offer arrived. However, the available opening was in the Tool Design Department, and the pay was a measly $16 a week. Still, Louis decided to accept.

Shortly after starting work, Louis was warned, "Watch out for M. C." He had no idea what this meant until a wiry man with a stern look spied him examining one of the new machines. Louis explained that he wanted to learn how it operated with such precision. His answer satisfied the listener, who turned out to be Mario Caruso. That's how Louis met the inimitable "M. C."

Not long after, Caruso provided Louis with an opportunity to show off his

35

Lawrence Parker supervised some of the first projects that Louis carried out at Lionel. These included designing the employee newsletter and illustrating a brochure for the Lion-Eds toys.

talents. Federal officials had demanded that a set of military plans be retouched, and Louis volunteered for the job. Caruso furnished him with what he needed and was astonished when he completed the task in just a few hours.

Word of his skills spread quickly. In 1943, when Lionel's production of precision instruments earned the "M" Award of Merit from the United States Maritime Commission, Louis was asked to help the firm commemorate that event. Philip Marfuggi, editor of the employee newsletter, *Lionel Lines,* selected Louis to oversee production of a special edition.

Meanwhile, Caruso and Parker requested that Louis illustrate material advertising the line of wood toys they hoped Lionel would market. That brochure and other pieces of promotional literature Louis put together more than satisfied the works manager. Then, before leaving Lionel in October 1944, Caruso decided that the company should enter the growing field of photo reproduction. To organize a new department, he named Louis Melchionne.

DEPARTMENT 16

Louis accepted the challenge of starting the Reproduction Department. He made sure that Department 16, as it was designated, received the equipment to reproduce blueprints and other documents for engineering and tool design, among its other jobs. By 1949, reported *All Aboard at Lionel* (the renamed employee newsletter), "A varityper, ditto duplicator, high-speed offset press and folding machine constituted the department's printing equipment." In addition, a Photostatting camera had been installed. Everything seemed to be going well, even though "M. C." had departed and Joseph Bonanno had demanded that Department 16 be placed under his purview.

Bonanno, who found it difficult to trust others to meet his own high standards, occasionally made life hard for Louis. Generally, though, the two got along, and Bonanno came to respect his associate's attention to detail as they worked together on the Electronic Control Set, first cataloged in 1946. For

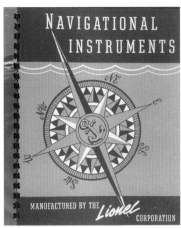

During the Second World War, Louis was responsible for materials that announced Lionel's production of naval instruments.

that experimental outfit, Louis contributed the color-coded decals on each freight car as well as artwork for the instruction sheets.

Friendlier than Bonanno was Frank Pettit, who called on Louis to assist with special projects, including the no. 2332 GG1. For this model of the Pennsylvania Railroad's streamlined electric locomotive, Louis labored on the elaborate striping and keystone heralds. A special machine had to be built that rolled gold stripes onto each model.

Not too long after, Pettit developed the no. 132 Passenger Station using plans that Louis provided. Experience as a tool designer enabled Louis to conceive of this large, all-plastic accessory and show how it could be manufactured without painting.

Louis remembers as well contributing to some of the common rolling stock released after the war. For example, he designed all the lettering and emblems that were heat-stamped on the no. 2454 Baby Ruth boxcar and took care of the decals decorating the nos. 2465 and 2555 Sunoco tank cars.

RELATIONS WITH MR. COWEN

Ask anyone who worked at Lionel about J. L. Cowen, and they'll have no trouble sharing memories. Louis is no different. "Mr. Cowen was a wonderful man, always stopping by my department when on his regular visits to the factory. He would ask what I was doing and then listen as I explained."

Sometime in the late 1940s, Cowen asked Louis to draw silhouettes of passengers in order to improve the appearance of the no. 2625 heavyweight Pullman car. Louis devised a way to attach decaled silhouettes to opaque paper. Cowen was pleased until he noticed the illustration of a conductor holding his hands in front of his body. A little imagination was all it took to recognize that Louis had unwittingly shown the conductor in a rather unflattering pose. Cowen roared, and Louis quickly saw his mistake.

Cowen's concern that his electric trains be wholesome toys came to light

Starting after the war, Louis was given a say in the design of Lionel's rolling stock and accessories. This stunning painting influenced the appearance of the no. 132 Passenger Station, first cataloged in 1949.

in a second incident that occurred about the same time. Lionel had long worked with businesses to promote products ranging from candy to gasoline. Louis designed freight cars and billboards for this purpose. So he wasn't surprised when Bonanno instructed him to decorate a refrigerator car for Ballantine Beer.

As Louis concentrated on getting Ballantine's three-ring emblem right, Cowen strolled by. He stared and stared at the drawing board, then exploded. "Lionel will never advertise products that aren't good for children," Cowen yelled. A chagrined Bonanno ordered Louis to get rid of the car.

TECHNICAL LITERATURE

Before the Second World War, Lionel supplied its many authorized service stations with only limited information, usually just lists of replacement parts. The instruction sheets compiled for individual items were better, although the illustrations added to them weren't always clear or complete.

The problems were really twofold. First, Lionel contracted with outside vendors to lay out and print all of this technical literature. Invariably, information wasn't communicated and quality declined. Second, instruction sheets were treated as almost an afterthought. They weren't put together until orders for a new item had been taken and production was well along. Haste in finishing the sheets often led to more problems.

Changing this situation, Louis believed, required Lionel to handle the job internally. His department took care of the printing while upgrading the artwork and text. New technology was the key to improving the pictures. The

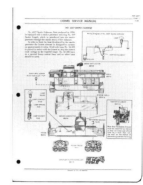

The Lionel Service Manual was a team effort, with Louis (center) working with his chief copywriters, Abe Kagan (left) and Thomas Festa (right), to be sure the text complemented the illustrations. The results, as shown, were exactly what experienced and novice Lionel enthusiasts needed.

technique for preparing service manuals was to place an item's parts on a Photostat machine. Here, Louis relied on Thomas Festa. Thanks to his father, Angelo Festa, a longtime general foreman at Lionel, Tom knew trains inside and out. Not only could he take them apart with ease, but he never flinched at cutting locomotive shells in half to expose the motor. Then Tom and Louis arranged the parts to look like an exploded-view drawing come to life.

Louis made Photostats of the parts on an especially thin paper, which he then carbonized on one side. Next, he had the Photostats traced, thereby creating a preliminary drawing ready to be inked. Once his department had finished with that step, Louis reduced the drawing to fit one of the standard sizes of paper being used for instruction sheets or the Lionel Service Manual.

WORKING WITH KAGAN

Now the accompanying text had to be written. Louis generally collaborated with Abe Kagan, a superb technical writer. The two were, at first glance, an unlikely pair, different in demeanor and appearance. But respect for each other's talents and a knack for compromise helped them thrive. Louis portrays them as a team, much like Richard Rodgers and Oscar Hammerstein II: "One of us provided the music, the other brought the lyrics."

Most often, Louis came in with the relevant illustrations and his partner wrote copy to fit. The two played ideas off each other, both eager to improve the other's work rather than disparage or reject it. When an instruction sheet was needed for a train set, Kagan dashed off the text and a track plan. Then Louis laid out the words and modified his drawings to accommodate whatever space remained.

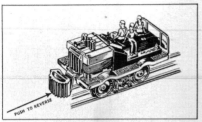
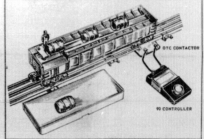

Louis also illustrated and designed dozens of instruction sheets.

Abe Kagan was outspoken, more so than Louis, but the pair felt a deep loyalty to each other. For Louis that meant overlooking the liberal political views of his colleague, whose opinions left some of Lionel's management uneasy. He remembers being questioned about Kagan by the Federal Bureau of Investigation during the mid-1950s, when fears of "un-American activities" were rampant. Wasting few words, Louis told an agent to leave his friend alone: "If Kagan's a communist, so am I!"

VARIED CONTRIBUTIONS

During The Lionel Corporation's glory years in the late 1940s and 1950s, Louis had more projects than he could handle then or recall now. And that's how he liked it. "I wasn't just a supervisor at Lionel," Louis states proudly, "but a working supervisor. My department was central to all activity, so I had my hands on everything." Yet he never gave anything short shrift. "Mr. Melchionne was so conscientious," Catherine Avella, his secretary, comments. "He always seemed worried about making a mistake and disappointing his superiors."

Curiously, for someone involved with decoration, Louis wasn't invited to participate in any discussions about the paint schemes and road names used on various Lionel trains. Therefore, he can't shed light on the fascinating paint samples that have surfaced. Neither was he consulted about the pastel tones that were chosen for the no. 1587S Lady Lionel (better known as the Girls' Set) released in 1957.

In other areas of decoration, though, Louis was Lionel's expert. The first step in the decorating process involved obtaining artwork from the railroad or business whose name or emblem was going to adorn an item. After reducing the artwork to fit an O or O27 gauge model, Louis had to make modifications so it looked realistic on a toy yet didn't cost too much to

Seeking ways to help Lionel, in the 1950s Louis tried to interest it in Spello, a word game he had created to amuse and teach his children.

mass-produce or take too long to apply. Sensible advice on these matters came from Walter Camuso, supervisor of the Methods Department. With that information, Louis recommended whether using decals or heat-stamping was best for applying details.

Custom decals became a specialty of his. Among those that Louis remembers designing were the stripes on the no. 2333 Santa Fe and New York Central F3 diesels. Later, when Lionel introduced the O27 Alco FA, Louis decorated it with the familiar blue and white herald of the Union Pacific. The General Motors emblems that embellish Lionel's early NW2 switchers were more of his handiwork, as was the Fairbanks-Morse insignia placed on all the magnificent O gauge Train Masters.

A more challenging task was designing boldly colored feathers to decorate the sides of Lionel's Western Pacific boxcars. Louis followed his usual steps when creating a decal for the no. 3474 operating car (new in 1952). The size of the feather and the fact that it had to stretch across a door as well as the entire side of the car gave Louis more than his share of headaches. Then he realized that guides had to be integrated into the boxcar's design so workers could easily affix the decal in the correct position. Patterns of rivets served this function on the 3474.

Two years later, when Lionel added a yellow-feather car to its 6464 series of larger boxcars, Louis had to rethink his plans. Decaling the no. 6464-100 Western Pacific boxcar would be expensive and inefficient. Instead, Louis advised the Engineering Department to rely on screen-printing for the feather and heat-stamping for the lettering.

If Louis could design feathers, then why not entire birds or, in the case of one car, chickens? Artwork of hens roosting and pecking was required for the no. 6434 Poultry Dispatch car, first offered in 1958, and Louis supplied

In the late 1950s, Louis contributed artwork for the no. 6434 Poultry Dispatch car and its operating twin (3434) as well as the no. 3435 Traveling Aquarium car.

whimsical yet realistic depictions. Lionel relied on the same illustrations for an operating version of that car, the no. 3434, in which a figure supposedly swept out chicken litter. Impressed by the effort Louis had put forth, Bonanno turned to him when Lionel needed colorful illustrations of fish and seaweed for its no. 3435 Traveling Aquarium car, cataloged from 1959 to 1962.

FINAL YEARS AT LIONEL

Louis admits that he never paid too much attention to what was happening at Lionel's headquarters in New York. The sales and advertising staffs rarely consulted him, and he admits he wasn't overly fond of Lawrence Cowen, president of the firm. Sadly, the independence this isolation sustained was shattered when Roy Cohn, a powerful lawyer and distant relative of J. L. Cowen, gained control of Lionel in 1959. "The company went into darkness," Louis observes. Watching as friends and associates such as Frank Pettit and Charles Giaimo lost their jobs, he wondered whether he would be among the next to go.

Somehow Louis survived for eight more years, continuing to design and print instruction sheets and an array of service manuals and bulletins. If anything, his responsibilities grew as Lionel struggled to expand its product line. Louis drew flags and pennants for road racing sets and navigational insignia to go with a plastic boat for children. He added illustrations to Lionel boxes and even revamped the company's logo in the mid-1960s. Louis surrounded the Lionel name with arrows chasing each other. The design was intended to suggest an electric train as well as the slot cars that Robert Wolfe, then president of Lionel, hoped would bolster the firm's image and finances.

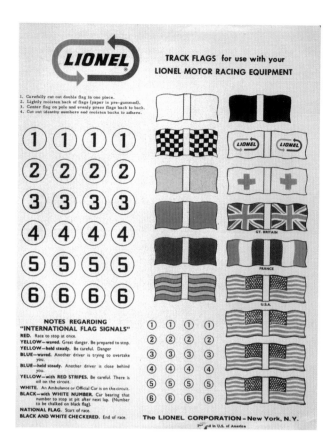

When Lionel diversified its toy line in the 1960s, Louis designed artwork for a road racing set. He also contributed the logo at the top of this leaflet.

Louis sensed that the company's downward slide was accelerating. Efforts to diversify Lionel's holdings were failing to bring in needed revenue. Louis knew all about what Cohn and Wolfe wanted to do, as he had put together a splashy brochure in 1961, *The Lionel Corporation: A New Force.* The photos looked impressive and the text made Lionel sound important, but Louis knew it was all show. "That's why," he chuckles, "I call that brochure, *Lionel: A New Farce!*"

In 1967, the number of people employed at the New Jersey factory dwindled until everyone, including Louis, was let go. He left saddened by how far Lionel had fallen, but not embittered. His optimistic view of life as well as his pleasant recollections of working at Lionel made that impossible. Instead, Louis parlayed his experience into a job at a local advertising agency, where he worked until he was well into his seventies.

Today, Louis and Phylis, his wife of more than 65 years, enjoy life and continue to look ahead. "I was lucky to work at Lionel during its greatest years," he says, "and I think I contributed to its success." Those of us who cherish Lionel trains have no doubts that Louis Melchionne contributed significantly to that company's legacy.

John DiGirolamo refined his engineering knowledge while working at Lionel, experience that helped him build Jerome Industries.

JOHN DIGIROLAMO

Adding Magic to Electric Trains

What has made Lionel trains special, even magical, to children and adults for nearly a century is their movement. Their colors surely dazzle, and their detail never fails to impress, but the fact that miniature locomotives can start and stop without having to be maneuvered by hand has always amazed onlookers. The reason, of course, is electricity. Household current sends power to motors inside models. Watching them move, first slowly and then faster and faster, thrills kids of all ages.

Credit for launching this revolution in the development of toy trains does not belong to Joshua Lionel Cowen. Even he never claimed to have invented the miniature electric train. But he did refine and popularize the concept and then promoted the use of electricity to illuminate models of stations and passenger coaches, to automatically stop and start trains, and to generate whistling and ringing sounds.

Throughout the late prewar and much of the postwar years, engineers labored at Lionel's factory to find new ways of using electricity to create magic in the firm's toy trains. The Electronics Laboratory was an exciting and secretive place. John DiGirolamo supervised a variety of projects during the 20 or so years he worked in the lab as assistant chief engineer. His recollections shed new light on the development of products at Lionel.

"LIONEL MAKES TRAINS?"

Unlike many former Lionel employees, who grew up in the shadow of its factory or played with its trains as youngsters, John DiGirolamo was unfamiliar with the company when he applied for a job there. He had more important matters on his mind in the spring of 1943. "I was getting

In the years immediately after the Second World War, George Jurasov (left) worked with John on projects relating to the development of new transformers and Magne-Traction.

ready to graduate from Columbia College in New York with a degree in mechanical engineering," John recalls. "I wanted to get a job at a place where my position would enable me to get some practical experience before I was drafted. After all, there was a war going on! So I picked up a copy of the *Newark Star-Ledger* and noticed an advertisement for an opening at Lionel."

The name meant nothing to John. There weren't many toys, certainly not electric trains, in the poor, predominantly Italian, neighborhood in Jersey City, New Jersey, where he grew up. "My family arrived from Italy in 1930, when I was only ten years old," John relates. "The Depression hit everybody hard, and my family had next to nothing left when we finally got to America. There was no way we could afford a train set." In the face of hardships, John pushed himself to excel. He compiled an outstanding record as a student and athlete at James J. Ferris High School, graduating with honors in 1939. That record then earned him a scholarship to play football at Columbia under its legendary coach, Lou Little.

Everything John read about in the ad and saw during his initial interview was military products. Lionel had been awarded several contracts by the armed forces and was busy producing telegraph keys for the Army Signal Corps and binnacles, alidades, compasses, and other navigational instruments for the Navy. A surprise awaited him as he was ushered into the office of Joseph Bonanno. "In back of his desk was a picture of a toy train," John explains. "I couldn't figure out why, so I asked the secretary. 'Don't you know where you are?' she responded. What do you mean? Lionel makes trains in peacetime? She must have thought I was crazy!"

Of course, since Lionel was prohibited from manufacturing any electric trains during the war, it scarcely mattered what the firm's main business was. For now, it was one more producer of war materiel, and that was what Bonanno wanted his new assistant to emphasize. "Mr. Bonanno was the only true engineer at Lionel when I started," John states, "and with 1,700 people working there, he desperately needed help with the military work. He couldn't spare me, even to fight, which is why I received an industrial deferment for the remainder of the war."

Bonanno gave his new assistant responsibility for items being produced for the Signal Corps. Even before John had figured out where everything was located in the factory, he was designing and building test equipment for fast-acting as well as time-delayed re-

Not long after starting at Lionel, John met Theresa Ferrari, whom he married in 1947.

lays, contactors, and audio and power transformers. As important, Bonanno insisted that he move around the facility and observe what was happening in other departments. John spent plenty of time on the assembly lines, asking questions and troubleshooting problems. No wonder he felt confident in saying, "I learned about every aspect of industrial development and production during my years at Lionel."

STEPPING INTO A GREAT PLACE

"For a guy straight out of school, Lionel was a great place to be," John declares. As he talks about being there in the middle and late 1940s, it becomes clear that his education as an engineer had barely begun when he received his diploma from Columbia. During his first seven or eight years at Lionel, he gained innumerable insights into the world of electrical engineering and learned valuable lessons about working with others and mastering every aspect of a new project. The education he picked up would, years later, give him the confidence and capability to open his own firm.

His first, and in many ways most influential, teacher at Lionel was Joseph Bonanno. By the time John started working there in the summer of 1943, Bonanno had established a reputation as a brilliant engineer who had helped create a full line of top-quality O gauge trains and accessories, some of which were equipped with ingenious remote-control features. He was familiar with up-to-date processes of metal die-casting and plastics molding and was already turning his attention to such novel fields as powdered metallurgy. "Mr.

In the Engineering Department, John (left) learned a great deal from Morris Zion (center) and Joseph Bonanno (right).

Bonanno read three books and a dozen journals every night," John says without much exaggeration. "And he made it clear that he expected everybody else to keep up with him."

Maybe that was the problem. Few engineers in the country could have equaled Bonanno's appetite for research. His expectations were incredibly high, and he made no secret of his disdain and frustration with colleagues who failed to meet them. Bonanno had little use for most of the supervisors at Lionel, few of whom could boast of completing high school. Even other engineers were treated with a mix of impatience and indifference. Bonanno wanted them to devise and perfect new products that would benefit the firm, all the while never threatening his supremacy.

Reading the situation correctly, John tried to emulate his boss. "Mr. Bonanno was almost 20 years older than I was," he begins, "so we didn't have much in common and never socialized. But I had the utmost respect for his abilities and dedication to the company. I followed his example and studied related fields of engineering so I could obtain a firm grasp of areas that concerned Lionel." Initially, that meant concentrating on the production of military items; later, once peace returned, John focused on trains, particularly motors, relays, transformers, and accessories. In addition, he supplemented his education by enrolling at Newark College of Engineering, where he taught in the evenings between 1950 and 1960.

On a day-to-day basis, John talked often with other key people working under Bonanno. Morris Zion, born in Russia and educated in Italy, had come to America in 1939. Like Bonanno, he was conversant in a variety of engineering specialties. He did his best to acquaint John with everything he would need to know to improve the design of many military items. George Jurosov and John Salles, also educated in Europe and brought to Lionel by Mario Caruso, supplemented John's understanding of electronics, particularly when applied to toy trains. Salles, born in France and a veteran of colonial wars in Indochina and the Spanish Civil War, proved to be an exceptional teacher and good friend over the years.

By the early 1950s, John was in charge of one of the labs where new mechanisms and models were developed.

"I worked with some terrific people in my first years at Lionel, but maybe the best aspect was the philosophy there." The prevailing attitude, or "philosophy," according to John, was that production should be virtually self-sufficient. Once raw materials were purchased, everything necessary to transform them into finished goods ought to be done within the confines of Lionel's factory. The tools and dies required to mass-produce items ranging from enormous binnacles to O27 gauge locomotives should be designed and made there. Further, diverse industrial processes had to be mastered and organized: die-casting and stamping metal, compression- and injection-molding plastics, coil winding, plating, painting, heat- and rubber-stamping, and so on. Finished pieces were then packaged and shipped from Hillside.

"Nobody carried out all these processes as well as Lionel did in the 1940s and '50s," John insists, adding that a desire for self-sufficiency is rarely heard from current manufacturers. And with good reason. "Back then, you couldn't rely on suppliers and subcontractors, not when you had tight deadlines to make with a seasonal market like Lionel's. Keep in mind, we had to wait until Toy Fair in the late winter to find out what we would be making. Then we had to rush into production to fill the orders for Christmas."

The fact that Lionel could produce so much from start to finish each year is, John emphasizes, a tribute to excellent management and the outstanding efforts of many hundreds of hard-working men and women. He has only the highest praise for the ability of Mario Caruso and Charles Giaimo, who succeeded

Caruso as works manager, and such loyal, far-seeing assistants as Tom Pagano, Anthony LaFauci, and Peter Giannotta. Working in a factory that carried out so many steps in manufacturing toy trains ensured that John would gain first-hand knowledge of how electricity could be put to work to instill magic in Lionel's line.

TESTING, TESTING

Observing how Lionel was making communication equipment for the armed forces led John into the field of testing. Bonanno wanted him to improve the quality of Lionel's work and all but guarantee that the items turned out worked reliably. Right from the start, therefore, John was asked to combine his background in mechanical engineering with informal training in electrical engineering. He rose to the challenge and proved to his superiors that he could be a valuable member of the team.

The same interest in seeing that Lionel's trains operated smoothly prodded John to focus on transformers immediately after the war. Perhaps the biggest project going on in the Engineering Department was Bonanno's pet, the Electronic Control Set. This unprecedented experiment used radio frequency waves to operate a special train set, not to mention uncouple its cars and blow its whistle. The chief engineer did not select John to assist him; instead, Bonanno wanted him to work with Zion on improving transformers and all other electro-mechanical items used, such as relays, solenoids, circuit breakers, and motors.

John took off in two directions. One diverted his attention to the top of Lionel's line. Believing that the biggest sets needed a powerful, multiple-purpose transformer, he helped transform the mundane 250-watt Z into the legendary ZW in 1948. With its dual football-shaped controls, panoply of buttons and knobs, and glowing green and red lights, the ZW mesmerized youngsters. They dreamed of owning one of these monsters and being able to run as many as four trains on their layouts, all the while blasting whistles or reversing at the touch of a button. Thanks to its unique look and ample power (it was upgraded to 275 watts in 1950), the ZW remains a favorite of operators.

The other path John followed in the late 1940s guided him toward the low end of the line. Sales executives, fearful that inexpensive windup and electric trains marketed by Louis Marx & Co. were luring away customers, pushed for simpler trains than the O27 offerings Lionel cataloged. In response, engineers developed the Scout, which was first cataloged in 1948. Although the plastic-case motor in the steam engine was far from perfect and the plastic rolling stock lacked detail, salesmen breathed a sigh of relief. Once more they had undermined the competition.

The bare-bones Scout needed its own transformer, and John proved equal to the task. He contributed an elementary one, the 25-watt 1011, which featured only directional control. Meanwhile, he labored on a more important transformer, the no. 1033. That 90-watt source of power became a staple of the

As John recalls, the earliest designs for what became the 497 Coaling Station were created by the famous industrial designer Raymond Loewy.

O27 line from its debut in 1948 through 1956. As with all his work, John made sure his staff conducted plenty of tests on these midget transformers. That meant developing electrical equipment that inspectors in the Testing and Quality Control Departments used to test the 1033 and its mates.

The success of the 1033 made all the time and effort John had spent on the project worthwhile. He recalls the pride that filled him as he gained Bonanno's trust and respect. The bonus John had been hoping for came in 1950, when Bonanno appointed him supervisor of the Electronics Laboratory and delegated to him key duties, among them patent processing and product and technical suggestion review. The prestige of joining the product planning team and supervising preliminary model making also awaited him. For someone still in his twenties, John had advanced rapidly at Lionel. The next decade would only enhance his authority there.

MOVING FREIGHT FOR LIONEL

New challenges lay ahead in the 1950s. John already had proved his value to Lionel in strengthening its relationship with America's military. Over the coming years, particularly during the Korean War, he worked even more closely with government laboratories and purchasing departments, as he conducted the bidding on various projects. Once Lionel was awarded military contracts, John supervised all phases of the design and production. He broadened his knowledge of the line, yet never cut himself off from trains.

On the contrary, throughout the late 1940s, John tackled demanding though necessary projects that helped make Lionel's trains operate better. Besides improving transformers, he watched as the experiments that led to the development of Magne-Traction were performed under his jurisdiction in the Electronics Laboratory. No one could question the importance of assuring the quality of electronic components and analyzing the magnetism of wheels made of sintered iron. Still, this work lacked the excitement of being at the forefront of new product development. Fortunately for John, he was ready when the chief engineer asked him to try something new.

Bonanno insisted that John take a look at some of the accessories under consideration. For example, an updated version of the automatic gateman was on the drawing boards as Lionel approached its golden anniversary. More exciting was a new log loader, no. 364, which made its debut in 1948. This accessory differed from no. 164, Lionel's other log loader, in that it moved logs unloaded from a special freight car up a horizontal conveyor belt until they reached a platform, where they rolled into another waiting car. In 1952, designers created a similar accessory, no. 362, which depended on a vibrating mechanism to transport small barrels up a ramp.

With his friend and colleague, Patrick Tomaro Jr. (right), John raised a glass at one of the holiday gatherings held at Lionel in the 1950s.

Each of these accessories needed an inexpensive, hardworking motor that kids could use endlessly without the risk of its quitting. Bonanno, putting more trust in his associate, gave the assignments to John. Perhaps what persuaded him to do so were memories of how, just a couple of years after being hired, DiGirolamo had improved the mechanism by which cans were delivered on the no. 3462 Operating Milk Car. Pleased with his subordinate's progress, Bonanno thought he should take a look at the new accessories.

John started his tinkering with the gateman. This staple was being redesigned in the late 1940s, a process that included bolstering the solenoid so it operated better while being built for less. "Don't forget," he begins, "that cost was paramount. With the military work done during the war, you could spend a good amount on the mechanism to make sure it worked smoothly. But with toy train accessories, you had to keep expenses down. The motor had to be small and work all the time." The same principle influenced John's efforts to improve what he refers to as "the electro-mechanical" elements of the 364 Log Loader and 362 Barrel Loader.

Not long after, Bonanno requested that he assist efforts to develop a freight station on which figures appeared to move parcels. Frank Pettit, the firm's development engineer, had come up with plans for what became the 356 Operating Freight Station. The structure looked fine, and the concept of having baggage carts move in and out of the station on a belt captivated everyone. However, problems had arisen regarding the mechanism to be installed.

"Everything had to work smoothly," John explains, "otherwise, the effect was lost and kids were bound to be disappointed." After a lot of trial and error, he decided to revamp the vibrating mechanism Frank had developed for this accessory. John substituted a central vibrator coil for the pair of solenoids he says originally were installed. Now the two carts moved in and out of the station with hardly a hitch. The effect was spectacular, and everyone in the Engineering Department came away smiling. Grateful because John's efforts really made it possible for Lionel to release the accessory, Bonanno put John's name on the patent that was awarded the inventor of the freight station.

Once John had begun aiding with the development of accessories, he never wanted to surrender that aspect of his job and went on to receive six patents for electro-mechanical components and products he designed at Lionel. He can remember contributing to several large and somewhat complex items later in the 1950s, including the nos. 342 Culvert Pipe Loader, 464 Lumber Mill, and 3356 Operating Horse Car (all new in 1956). He supervised the skilled work required to adjust their motors so freight was moved in a realistic manner that enhanced the magic spell Lionel hoped to weave.

HELP FROM OUTSIDE

The prevailing notion of self-sufficiency at Lionel generally applied as well to the toy trains and accessories developed for its line. Staff engineers, especially Pettit, were expected to devise novel operating pieces each year. That the line kept growing testified to the depth of their imagination and skill. Of course, this didn't stop outsiders from mailing in models of new-fangled accessories. Most of the time, those submissions ended up in the trash, with only a polite response from Lionel. Occasionally, however, DiGirolamo and his associates walked away impressed and sought to buy all rights to the inventions.

John's favorite example was the milk car. Under various numbers and in different forms, it became a landmark in Lionel's history and millions were sold. "The idea for the milk car reached us right after World War II," John recalls. "It came from a fellow in upstate New York named Richard Smith. He was around 40 years old and somewhat mentally and physically disabled; his wife kept him busy with toy trains. He liked to tinker and eventually came up with a working model of the milk car, with the figure appearing to push milk cans out of the car. His wife made sure we paid them plenty."

Waiting for worthwhile projects like Smith's to reach Lionel proved frustrating to sales and engineering executives. And they didn't want to count on their staffs to fill in any gaps: "It's too demanding to expect your people to be geniuses every year," John complains. So Bonanno started soliciting ideas. The most fascinating of his plans emerged early in the 1950s. As John tells the story, his boss went right to the top, approaching Raymond Loewy, the acclaimed industrial designer, about creating an accessory. Specifically, Bonanno wanted an O gauge coal loader from the man credited with, among other triumphs, the Pennsylvania Railroad's redesigned GG1 electric and Coca-Cola's distinctive bottle.

Loewy didn't shy away from the assignment. Instead, he conceived of a novel method for loading and dumping the chunks of Bakelite that masqueraded as coal in Lionelville. "After a month," John continues, "he submitted a single drawing and a bill for $6,000." The effort wasn't adequate, and the expense was far beyond what Lionel could afford. As a result, Loewy's career with Lionel ended shortly after it began. Luckily for the company and its customers, Lionel could take his idea to the bank. Model makers got right to work and produced the unique 497 Coaling Station, which was cataloged from 1953 through 1958.

More fulfilling for Lionel was the arrangement Bonanno worked out with Kenneth Van Dyck, a designer whose family the chief engineer had known for years. Van Dyck, originally based in Philadelphia before moving to Westport, Connecticut, and establishing his own firm, agreed to provide Lionel with as many designs as he could for a price substantially lower than what Loewy had charged. Even better, he was willing to travel to New Jersey each week to discuss his designs with the engineering staff.

"This guy [Van Dyck] was great to work with," John states. "Morris Zion, Joe Bonanno, and I would sit down with him and tell him what we wanted to do. He would listen and then come up with beautiful design renditions of all kinds of new trains and accessories." From Van Dyck's mind came plans for novel motorized units, including the nos. 44 U. S. Army Mobile Missile Launcher, 54 Ballast Tamper, and 3927 Track Cleaning Car. He also had a hand in the creation of operating rolling stock, notably, the nos. 3376 Bronx Zoo, 3512 Ladder Co., and 6650 I. R. B. M. Launcher. Kenneth Van Dyck's efforts, like Richard Smith's, demonstrate the significance of outside contributions to Lionel's success during the postwar era.

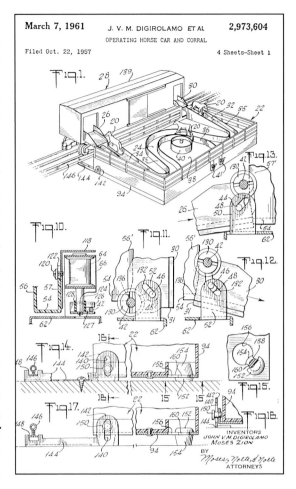

Among the items for which John received patents while at Lionel, the 3356 Operating Horse Car and Corral may be the most familiar to collectors.

THE BENEFITS OF CHANGE

As the 1950s closed, John could look back with pride at how high he had risen at Lionel and the many projects to which he had contributed. By 1957, he had been promoted again, this time to supervisor of the Research and Development Laboratory. He continued to administer the Electronics Laboratory, along with the Test Equipment, Production Engineering, and Technical Writing Departments. Under his management were a number of other engineers, not to mention designers and technicians. Three of these men became John's partners in a special group that carried out product evaluation, prepared lines for mass-production of newly approved items, and did whatever troubleshooting was required. He was especially good at breaking in assistants whom he recruited fresh out of college. His future with Lionel looked bright indeed.

Then came two dramatic changes that jeopardized John's chances for further advancement. The sudden death of Morris Zion in 1959 left a vacuum directly below Bonanno. Competition for Zion's position as assistant to the chief engineer was inevitable, though John thought the job should belong to him. Kenneth Perry, roughly his contemporary in age but with less experience at Lionel, campaigned for the pro-

Encouraged by the knowledge and experience he had acquired at Lionel, John left in the early 1960s to found Jerome Industries.

motion, which would entitle him to oversee the draftsmen and model makers.

The bigger shock occurred in the autumn of 1959, when J. L. Cowen sold control of the firm to Roy Cohn. The sale attracted a good deal of attention in the business world; people either respected or reviled Cohn because he had aided Senator Joseph McCarthy during a televised investigation of subversion in the military. The same extreme reactions met the news that Cohn now controlled Lionel. For many members of the old guard, his ascendancy bred fear— and rightly so. A few lost their jobs immediately; others handed in their resignations over the next year.

John had no intentions of leaving and actually saw opportunities for himself once Cohn took over as chairman of the board and appointed General John Medaris as president in 1960. He approved of their efforts to expand Lionel's role in producing instruments, motors, and other items for the armed forces and aerospace industry. Likewise, he supported plans to acquire a number of small firms in those fields as a way of compensating for the decline in sales of Lionel's electric trains and science-oriented toys.

By contrast, Perry mistrusted Cohn and wanted to quit. He soon secured a job offer that promised a nice raise. Cohn, unhappy about losing a top engineer just when he hoped to expand Lionel's presence in the field of electronics, countered that offer and listened as Perry presented his case to take over Zion's position and have DiGirolamo work under him. Complicating matters still further was what to do with Patrick Tomaro Jr., who was in charge of research and development for all government projects.

Cohn consulted Bonanno, whose expertise and value to Lionel preserved his authority. Rather than favor one of the younger men at the risk of alienating the others, they elected to have DiGirolamo, Perry, and Tomaro share power. Such an arrangement was guaranteed to be short-lived, thanks to the different interests and egos of those involved. "Ken and Pat got more involved in the toy train part," John explains, "and I was more involved in the industrial and military aspect."

Before long in the early 1960s, John was refining his job to focus on marketing instead of engineering. He concentrated on serving as a liaison between Lionel's engineering division and prospective customers. In this capacity he supplied information on its engineering and production abilities and provided technical information, established costs, estimated pricing, and negotiated contracts on assorted commercial and military products. Difficult as all his changing responsibilities might have been for John, they would pay enormous dividends for him in the coming years.

First, however, he had to endure one more trial at Lionel. In 1964, as he was preparing to take over administration of the company's diverse electronics subsidiaries, a challenger emerged among the executives at one of those companies. The sales manager at Telerad insisted that he be entrusted with running the division. John, learning that he was going to be passed over, resigned. Within a few weeks, he had established Jerome Industries in Elizabeth to gain a foothold in the burgeoning consumer electronics field. Joseph DiTrolio, an old friend equally dissatisfied with his treatment by Lionel, worked with John, and they built a strong, profitable business.

LESSONS LEARNED

At Jerome, John put into practice virtually everything he had learned in 21 years at Lionel about industrial designing, troubleshooting, marketing, and testing. Convinced that Lionel should all but abandon its train and toy lines, he had no qualms about purchasing its line of children's phonographs and producing them himself. "Lionel lacked the resources to adequately promote the Spear phonographs," he states. "We bought them and put the line on solid ground."

John confesses that he misjudged the appeal of some of Lionel's toys. Asked by Bonanno whether the company ought to invest in the tooling necessary to build slot cars, he shrugged off the notion as a fad that would quickly pass. Overall, however, John thinks Lionel should have stopped producing science toys and all except the top-of-the-line train sets to concentrate on electronic components for the armed forces and home appliances. That formula has brought success to Jerome Industries for more than three decades.

"What I've accomplished at Jerome," John concludes, "was made possible by what I learned from watching and listening to people at Lionel. Joe Bonanno, John Salles, Morris Zion: these were the greatest teachers you could have. But the key to my success was my own initiative and drive. Without those traits, I might have stuck it out at Lionel until the bitter end and never built up my own firm."

Jerry and Harriet Lamb smile as they recall the good years at Lionel.

JERRY LAMB
Hitting the Road for Lionel

Times were rough in the months after the Japanese surrender ended the Second World War. Many thousands of soldiers and sailors were returning to the United States, eager to find a job, settle down, and reap the benefits of civilian life. With so many men looking for work in 1945 and 1946 and the nation's economy only slowly switching over to the production of consumer goods, not every veteran was hired as quickly as he wanted.

Jerry Lamb knew the frustration many former servicemen were feeling. Although only 21 in 1946, he had fought with the Marines as they island-hopped across the Pacific toward Japan. Back with his family in Queens, he was ready for quieter times. His father had a friend at Lionel, and Jerry soon found himself being interviewed for a sales position.

"Why not take a job at Lionel?" Jerry asked himself. He had played with electric trains as a youngster and thought he might enjoy himself. Besides, he discovered that he wasn't the only veteran there. Three other guys in their twenties, all of whom had been overseas, joined the sales force right after the war and, like Jerry, stayed into the 1960s. Their experiences in New York and their sales territories add humor and insight to the Lionel story.

Lionel's sales staff posed in the New York showroom in 1947. Arthur Raphael and Sam Belser, mentors to all the younger men, sit in the middle of the front row. Jerry and his good friends Joe Mariamson, Myles Walsh, Bill Gaston, and Jack Kindler take their places in back.

TRAINING EACH OTHER

Myles Walsh arrived first. A graduate of the University of Notre Dame who had served in the Army Air Corps, he signed on right as the rush for electric trains was erupting in late 1945 and Lionel was redeveloping its sales staff. His hard work brought the reward he had desired. Myles was given his own sales territory, starting in the spring of 1946. He became the company's man in New England and much of New Jersey. Traveling for much of the year, he received orders for product, showed retailers how to repair trains and accessories, and built an array of displays for shop windows.

The other three new guys were hired in 1946. As explained in Chapter 8, Jack Kindler was hired late in the year as a demonstrator. Rather than meet with wholesalers or promote Lionel trains in other states, he made the company's New York showroom his base of operations. There, he showed customers how to operate a train set and sketched rudimentary track plans to encourage them to purchase track, switches, and accessories. In time, Jack moved on to creating special store displays, pushing Lionel on television programs, and overseeing the gigantic layouts built for the showroom.

Bill Gaston and Jerry Lamb were recruited as potential salesmen. They were not expected to travel far beyond the borders of New York City. Instead, they were designated "trainee juniors" and, like Kindler, were posted at Lionel's showroom. There, Bill and Jerry talked with buyers for department and chain stores and advised individual customers. They also were responsible for running the large layouts that were the centerpiece of the showroom, either the magnificent T-rail layout built before the war or the so-called Panorama Layout, which replaced it toward the end of 1946.

Those first few years at Lionel were an education for Jerry and Bill. Fortunately, they had some excellent teachers. Arthur Raphael, the executive vice-president and national sales manager, made sure the newcomers learned the ins and outs of the current line. His assistant, Sam Belser, shared tips on the best ways to sell trains and conduct themselves with wholesalers. Tougher to get along with were Irving Shull, who managed the Service Department, and Jimmy Santangelo, who administered the stock room. They expected the new guys to learn the ropes on their own and quit pestering them with questions. Of course, the finest mentor someone at Lionel could have was Joshua Lionel Cowen, the firm's founder and chairman of the board.

"J. L. was a prince among princes," Jerry remembers. "He was like my grandfather." What drew them together? Jerry admits that his combat experience had left him fretful. "It took me a couple of years to get over what I'd seen." Cowen noticed how thin and tense Jerry was and suggested that the young man see a physician, but not just any one. "Pop, as I called him, told me to stop by his own doctor on Park Avenue, which I did. That had to cost money, but he took care of everything. J. L. was just a beautiful guy, and I loved him."

Regaining his health and composure, Jerry began to relax and have fun. On one hot summer day, he helped Bill and Myles line up some chairs on one side of the showroom and arrange enormous floor fans on both sides. Then they pretended they were flying a plane on a bombing raid with all the appropriate sound effects. Surprised by the shenanigans, the older salesmen couldn't help doubling over in laughter as the veterans played.

Meanwhile, Bill and Jerry became close friends. "We taught each other," Jerry recalls with a grin. "Billy had been hired a month before I was, and he broke me in. He was the one that showed me the difference between O gauge and O27." Both of them had to learn fast, as droves of people were flocking to the showroom during the holiday seasons of 1946 and 1947. The demand for electric trains was sweeping New York. Bill and Jack, Myles and Jerry were there to witness the spectacle and take orders from an enthusiastic public.

HITTING THE ROAD

Early in 1948, with their training period over, Bill and Jerry were promoted. Each was sent outside New York to sell Lionel's product line of electric trains, construction and chemistry sets, and Airex fishing equipment to regional distributors and leading retailers. Previously, the two had ventured beyond the showroom only occasionally for what Jerry refers to as "missionary work." This typically amounted to nothing more than meeting with the owners of hardware and appliance stores in various boroughs of New York City in hopes of convincing them to stock Lionel trains around Christmas. The best of these excursions took Bill and Jerry out to Long Island, where they could sneak off to the beach for relaxation.

Bill Gaston (front) and Jerry represented Lionel at the Merchandise Fair, a major trade show held in Philadelphia in June 1948.

But once Raphael and Belser felt confident that the newcomers were familiar with the line, they sent them on the road. That initially meant traveling with one of the experienced salesmen to learn how to handle Lionel's accounts. At the time, five of the men working out of New York were responsible for the entire East Coast, reaching customers from Maine to Florida and as far west as Ohio and Texas. The rest of the United States was handled by representatives from the company's sales offices in Chicago and San Francisco.

Leading the way in the East were Larry Young and Joe Mariamson. These two old cronies had started with Lionel back in 1925 and 1936, respectively. They were colorful characters, gents who loved to spin yarns about the old days, mingle with the celebrities who stopped by the showroom, and enjoy some of the finer things in life, such as steaks, cigars, and whiskey. Next came Joe Malcolm, who had worked his way up from the Service Department. He tended to limit his travels to the New York vicinity. Myles Walsh concentrated on New England, while William Alpern and Bill Nicholls took care of the western and southern sections of Lionel's vast eastern territory.

To find places for Bill and Jerry, the region was cut up still further. Gaston handled parts of New York and northern New Jersey with Malcolm, while Jerry assisted Mariamson in Ohio, Pennsylvania, Kentucky, and West Virginia. Just handling the first two states was an incredible task for one man, as the number of stores carrying Lionel trains was enormous. Before long, thanks to his winning personality and diligence, Jerry was on his own.

Jerry (front, left) joined other members of the New York office at Lionel's factory to celebrate its golden anniversary. Standing in the center are Jack Kindler (left) and Myles Walsh (right)

LEARNING FROM THE MASTERS

It was Mariamson, with his wisecracking, superstitious ways, who proved to be Jerry's finest teacher. Joe was the quintessential salesman. The key to success? "Believe the product you sell is the best in the world," he answered. Sales was all he knew, even before he arrived at Lionel as the Depression was winding down. Joe became proficient at demonstrating and selling Lionel, then left the firm during the war. He returned in 1945 and resumed his position at the top, handling the large urban sprawl to the west of New York.

A delight to travel with, Joe took Jerry under his wing and shared everything he knew about sales. His protégé learned that being a successful salesman meant, first of all, "knowing your product inside and out." Then you had to know "the Gilbert product [American Flyer S gauge trains] inside and out, their strengths and weaknesses. We didn't have to worry about Hafner or Marx because they weren't in the same league as Lionel."

Mariamson emphasized the necessity of trusting your distributors, as well. "Learn what his problems are and the needs of his family, and do your best to resolve them." However, knowledge of the product and familiarity with the customer were only the beginning. "How you talked and dressed was equally important to Joe," Jerry emphasized.

"When I got out of the Marine Corps," he added, "I used to buy functional shoes that were tough and wore well. Joe would tan the hell out of me about that because those shoes simply weren't attractive. I remember one time, after we called on an account in a Pittsburgh store, Joe took me down to the shoe department and helped me pick out the kind of shoes I needed to look my best.

At the Toy Knights banquet in 1954, Jerry and Harriet Lamb (right) sat next to Alan and Rose Ginsburg. Continuing to the left were Ed Zier (Lionel comptroller), Jack Caffrey, Joe Mariamson, and Sam Belser (standing).

Then he paid for them. From there, he guided me to the men's department, and I tried on a nice suit. 'You like that suit?' Joe asked. 'I love it, but it's too expensive,' I told him. Didn't matter; he paid for it anyway.

"Joe was just a sweetheart. He was probably the most important thing that happened to me in the toy business. Nobody at Lionel was closer to me in all the years I worked there. When my wife, Harriet, would join me for the Toy Knights banquet during Toy Fair, Joe always made sure we had a nice room at the Waldorf-Astoria Hotel. He arranged with the manager to have a bottle of champagne and a bouquet of flowers in the room. He knew the manager. Hell, Joe knew everybody in New York!"

During what can be called Jerry's apprentice years, he occasionally followed Joe Malcolm or Myles Walsh through their territories. "Mal taught me to never, ever appear nervous or walk into a buyer's office unprepared. Even your body language can give you away. Joe told me, 'That guy has no time to waste on someone who doesn't know who he is or what he needs.'"

Walsh impressed upon Jerry the importance of being courteous and cooperative with all distributors, no matter how small their operation. "Maintain a close and friendly association with Lionel dealers," he advised. That's the reason Myles went out of his way to design displays for his customers and be sure they had a steady supply of the products they wanted.

From Mariamson and Walsh, Jerry learned the fundamental lesson that selling, however grueling, offered its own rewards. "You never run into two identical situations, and you get to meet a variety of people," Myles pointed out in a profile published in the February 1952 issue of *All Aboard at Lionel*.

Members of the New York sales staff assembled prior to the 1954 American Toy Fair (clockwise from lower left): Larry Young, Joe Malcolm, Bill Gaston, Robert Rudolph, Ronald Saypol, Jerry Lamb, Joe Mariamson, and Myles Walsh.

If you liked the travel and enjoyed the camaraderie, being a Lionel salesman could be the perfect job.

THE BEST OF TIMES

For most of his first ten years at Lionel, Jerry felt that nothing he could do for a living could be as enjoyable. Sure, being on the road for seven or eight weeks at a stretch in the spring and autumn was tough, especially as his family was growing. But everywhere he went Jerry, as a representative of what was recognized as the leading player in the toy business, was treated like royalty.

One of the highlights of each year was the unveiling of the new product line at the annual American Toy Fair in New York. To be sure, Jerry and other members of the sales force had little or no say in what was added or dropped from the line. Instead, Raphael and Belser, along with Joseph Bonanno, Lionel's chief engineer, worked with J. L. and Lawrence Cowen on that part of the business. However, the line was so popular that Jerry and his cohorts couldn't have cared less about not being consulted. Besides, he laughs, "our ideas weren't always the greatest. I tried to convince Larry [Cowen] to make a model of a New York subway train. I was sure it would be a great seller. Finally, Larry said that it would do well in New York. 'But who the hell would buy it in Los Angeles or Detroit or Chicago?' he asked me. And he was right!"

Instead, Jerry, Bill, and the other salesmen were content to be dazzled by the new items being introduced each year. Jerry points to the no. 773 Hudson steam engine cataloged in 1950 as a personal favorite. "We [the salesmen] really pushed for that one, and we were thrilled when it came out. It looked especially great pulling the old heavyweight [Madison] cars. Somehow, though, Lionel never gave the Hudson the attention it deserved, and it was overshadowed by the introduction of Magne-Traction on other engines."

Another train Jerry remembers fondly was one he called "The Super Chief." Of course, he's referring to Lionel's gorgeous O gauge model of the Santa Fe's F3 diesel and the extruded aluminum streamlined passenger cars it pulled. Those beauties, first cataloged in 1952, were popular with customers throughout the nation. Even in places like Ohio, home to New York Central and not Santa Fe motive power, the warbonnet schemes of Lionel's nos. 2333 and 2343 F3s were favorites. And what happened in Ohio had taken on significance for Jerry.

When his unofficial apprenticeship ended, Jerry believed it was only a matter of time before he was awarded his own sales territory. Meanwhile, Joe Mariamson had requested that he be allowed to cut back on his travel and concentrate on markets closer to New York City. He was switched to Michigan, upstate New York, and eastern Pennsylvania. The rest of the Keystone State as well as much of Ohio became Jerry's responsibility. Assisting him in Ohio was Bill Nicholls, who handled the western part of the state until he left for The A. C. Gilbert Co. in 1953. Then Ohio belonged exclusively to Jerry.

SIGNS OF TROUBLE

Trying to fill the ever-increasing orders of wholesalers and retailers, building 4 x 8-foot displays for store windows, even helping get electric trains on television shows hosted by Arthur Godfrey and Robert Q. Lewis—the early 1950s were wonderful years to be at Lionel. "We were number one in the toy business; no one doubted that. At Toy Fair, buyers had to walk from 200 Fifth Avenue, where all the other companies were represented, over to our showroom if they wanted to see our new line. And they did it! Even the salesmen for American Flyer were nice because they knew we were on top."

All the same, warnings began to appear that the future might not be so bright. Arthur Raphael's death in June of 1952 disrupted the sales department. Sam Belser nurtured hopes of succeeding his boss, but Lawrence Cowen elected to bring in an outsider, Alan Ginsburg, to serve as executive vice president.

While some employees view Ginsburg in a sympathetic light, Jerry doubts that he understood the strength of Lionel's traditional product line. He criticizes Ginsburg for ignoring toy wholesalers while trying to bolster Lionel's reputation in the hobby industry. Further, Jerry believes that Ginsburg and Larry Cowen promoted items that had little sales potential and proved to be abysmal failures, all in order to broaden the appeal of electric trains. Jerry cites the no. 1587S Lady Lionel as one of the biggest mistakes they made.

Ginsburg and the younger Cowen also hurt the company when they were slow to respond to the rise of discount houses. Fair trade laws were challenged

In the late 1950s, Jerry (right) assisted Jack Caffrey at Lionel's office in Chicago. They showed off the HO line at a hobby show.

by enterprising firms that wanted to slash prices on train sets and accessories. To support the major distributors as well as the small retailers that had long sold Lionel trains at the prices specified in the annual catalog, top management called out its lawyers to restrain various discount firms. Even worse from Jerry's perspective, they ordered him and others on the sales force to avoid dealing with those firms. This strategy weakened sales and prevented Lionel from infiltrating new markets in the mid-1950s.

Another worrisome sign was the way Lionel finally entered the HO scale market in 1957. Jerry recalls trying to persuade Larry Cowen to develop a line of HO trains for several years, only to be told that Lionel was strictly a toy company. "This," Jerry complained, "from the guy who pushed Lionel to sell fishing gear and a camera!" Of course, hobbyists had been disparaging Lionel trains for so long that Jerry thinks Larry simply was responding defensively.

"Anyway, after spending years insisting that HO wouldn't last and was a flash in the pan, Larry suddenly changes his mind. Now Lionel can't get into the HO field fast enough. So instead of taking the time to develop its own trains, we quickly make a contract with Rivarossi in Italy to manufacture HO trains that we'll sell." From a salesman's point of view, the actions taken by Lionel didn't make sense. With Raphael dead and J. L. Cowen more or less retired by 1957, the golden years seemed over, and Jerry couldn't help worrying that Ginsburg and Larry Cowen lacked the brilliance, dedication, and insights that the company needed to thrive in a declining market.

HEAD SOUTH AND MOVE ON

By the late 1950s, Bill Gaston and Jerry Lamb were fixtures at Lionel. They were among the firm's best and most experienced salesmen. Joe Malcolm was managing the showroom, and Joe Mariamson was cutting back his time on the road. Another old-timer, Larry Young, had retired in 1955, a move that opened a new opportunity for Jerry. During his final years at Lionel, Young had covered parts of the southeastern United States. After he quit, Jerry was asked to handle that region. Although he and his family (including six children) were settled on Long Island, Jerry liked the idea of trying something different. The Lambs moved down to Georgia, settling into a large house outside Atlanta.

Another good friend at Lionel was Jim Stewart (left) who worked at Lionel's San Francisco office before transferring to its Chicago showroom in 1960, which is about when this photograph was taken.

The change proved exhilarating for a while, but questions about Lionel's future lingered in Jerry's mind. When Roy Cohn gained control of the company in 1959, Jerry adopted a wait-and-see attitude. Soon, however, he found himself dumbfounded by Cohn's efforts to diversify the line and establish Lionel as a leader in the aerospace industry. He expressed skepticism about Ginsburg's plans to create a successful line of science toys and develop toys modeled after those identified by the public with The A. C. Gilbert Co. "Lionel bought Porter Chemical Co. so it could have chemistry sets that would rival Gilbert's," Jerry states. "Then it proceeded to destroy the company that Harold Porter had spent decades building."

In 1962, disgusted with what he saw going on, Jerry called his old friend, Joe Mariamson, then serving as sales manager for the trains and motor racing division. "I need to talk with you about what's happening. They're doing things all wrong," Jerry noted tersely, referring to Alan Ginsburg and Robert Wolfe, the president of the firm. Mariamson promised to arrange a meeting, where they could discuss Lionel's prospects. Jerry flew to New York and dashed over to Lionel's offices, only to learn that all three men were out of town. Stunned by this deception, Jerry walked out and returned to Atlanta.

"I told Harriet what they had done to me. I was furious. Then I started making inquiries, because I was ready to quit. Within a week I had an offer from Fisher-Price, which makes toys for young children. So I resigned from Lionel and spent many happy years with Fisher-Price. I never regretted my decision to leave Lionel."

With Jerry living in Atlanta and later Chicago and working in a different segment of the toy field, he eventually lost contact with his pals at Lionel.

By 1961, when this picture was snapped, Jerry was based in Atlanta. Lionel asked him to present a special layout to Jay Vassalotti, who not long before had been badly injured in a tornado.

Occasionally he talked with Gaston, but rarely heard from Walsh, Kindler, or Mariamson. All four of them stayed at Lionel, though its fortunes were declining and they must have felt anxious about the future. Jack Kindler left for AT&T in 1966, but the others hung on until Lionel dismissed them a year or two later. Mariamson eventually returned and worked for the company in the early 1970s, after it had been sold to General Mills.

Why Walsh or Gaston stayed at Lionel can't be determined. They must have seen the same warning signals that Jerry did. Perhaps their sense of loyalty to the company was too strong or they simply couldn't believe that Lionel would not survive. After leaving Lionel, they continued to sell different types of consumer goods, then retired. Both gentlemen died in the early 1980s. They, like Jerry Lamb, were vital parts of the postwar Lionel story. All three men sold the electric trains and accessories that added joy to the lives of so many children. We who played with those trains long ago remain indebted to them and the older salesmen who taught them.

Tony Gotto sits at a workbench at Donna Models, the plastics molding shop he operates with his sons.

TONY GOTTO

Preserving the Spirit of the Model Shop

Tony Gotto never played golf with Joshua Cowen. He doesn't hold a patent on one of Lionel's operating accessories and never sold or repaired O gauge trains. He had nothing to do with the layouts in the New York showroom. In fact, Tony remembers visiting the fabled office at 15 East 26th Street only once.

So why focus on his years at Lionel? The reason is simple: Tony Gotto embodies the spirit of Lionel. Even though he can't claim much contact with the firm's electric trains, Tony represents what fellow employees believe is Lionel's legacy. The factory in Hillside, New Jersey, served as a school, a fraternity house, and a gymnasium for Tony. He grew up there in virtually every sense, and he knows it. That's why Lionel is never far from his mind. "I owe everything I have to Lionel," Tony insists. To repay that debt, he does his best to help others learn what Lionel meant to the hundreds of people who punched in every day.

COMING BACK IN 1969

Among those who learned from Tony was Dick Brantsner. More than 25 years ago, after General Mills bought Lionel's train line, Dick came to New

Jersey to revive production. He met the handful of men still on the payroll. They taught him a great deal, but Dick wanted to learn more. "Talk to Tony Gotto," they advised.

Talking to Tony is flipping open the *Encyclopedia Lionelica*. He knew everyone at the factory and everything that was going on. In the 18 years after he joined Lionel in 1945, Tony not only gained a slew of friends; this street-smart guy from Newark acquired the knowledge he would use for a lifetime. When Brantsner came calling, Tony shared his knowledge.

Not long after Tony began working at Lionel in 1945, he was asked to pose as a "farm boy" with the Stock-Watch, one of the firm's new products.

And why not? At Lionel, Tony treated every supervisor as a professor and gained the knowledge and experience to launch his own business. He majored in model making, injection- and compression-molding, and toolmaking. His minors were bowling and wisecracking. No wonder he could explain the entire manufacturing process to Brantsner in a way that was precise, accurate, and funny as hell.

Once Tony started talking, it didn't take long to get to the story of how he'd arrived at Lionel as the Second World War was winding down. "A dumb 16-year-old kid," Tony described himself. Already big and strong, he thought he knew it all. So he cut classes to go to the movies and mixed with a tough crowd. "The principal at Central High School gave me a choice: quit or be tossed out." Tony walked. That's when life really began for him.

DROPPING IN TO LIONEL

Where else was he going to hang out but at home? That was not much of a solution, Tony recalls. "Pop was teed off because he wanted me to graduate and become something to somebody." Furious with Tony's nonchalance, his father ordered him to get a job. "Thank God my Aunt Jean happened to be at Lionel."

Jean Calcagno had spent several years at Lionel by 1945. Luckily for Tony, his aunt had enough pull to ask for a favor. She mentioned her nephew to Gus Ferri, who ran the model shop in the Engineering Department, and he conferred with Joseph Bonanno. Everything was set.

For Tony, the first days at the factory brought one surprise after another. He'd never stepped into a place so huge and bustling. However, Tony wasn't a stranger to the kinds of work going on. Assisting his father over the years, he had picked up rudimentary carpentry and electrical skills.

This burly kid with an attitude spent his first few weeks moving equipment in and out of storage. "Oh yeah," Tony laughs, "I was helping Lionel make the transition from war production to toy train manufacturing." Then he got tired of the heavy labor and was set to complain.

Maybe Gus Ferri could read minds. Sensing Tony's frustration, he assigned his new hand a few items to make for the model shop. Through trial and error, Tony learned to use jeweler's saws and other precision tools. By cleaning lathes, milling machines, and forges, he learned what each piece of equipment did and how it was

As an apprentice at Lionel, Tony learned to use many different machines in the factory's die-casting department, toolroom, and model shop.

designed. Little by little, Tony felt himself at home amid the clique of model makers, and they accepted this newcomer, so much younger than anyone else in the Engineering Department.

A WORLD OF ITS OWN

The model shop at Lionel was a place unto itself in which tradition and vanity shaped daily practices. Perhaps no other group at Lionel played so central a role in the successful production of each item as the model makers. They were aware of their importance, and they took pride in it and their training.

Model makers worked very closely with the other members of the Engineering Department to develop new products. After a new locomotive, car, or accessory was recommended, Bonanno had plans drawn up for it. If the suggested toy replicated something in existence, draftsmen based their plans on a blueprint of the full-sized piece. If it did not, they relied on a research model of wood or plaster that often came from Frank Pettit's lab. Using the preliminary plans, modelers constructed a prototype more polished and complete than that earlier model.

The purpose of the prototype was to enable the Tool Design Department to determine whether any existing tools could be used to mass-produce the new item and what types of new ones would have to be developed. If new molds and dies were necessary, the prototype assumed greater importance, especially if that tooling was going to be made by an outside vendor.

In creating such prototypes, model makers had to work quickly yet precisely.

Tony found a home among the model makers working at Lionel in the late 1940s (left to right): Joseph Bonanno, Rocco Grieco, Rudy Hauptmann, Morris Zion, Heinz Wiesener, Emil Albert, Rudy Heller, William Surerus, Gus Ferri, and August Juch. Kneeling in front is Rocco Nisivoccia.

Each model had to show all the details of the proposed toy. It had to capture the features of the new item, reveal any potential flaws, and convey to tool-makers exactly what was required for mass-production. The individuals making these models were, without question, among the most talented and least heralded characters in the fascinating story of Lionel.

At the top stood Gustave Ferri. Supervisor of the model shop, he exercised authority in an easy-going manner without letting his men lose sight of the fact that their models had to meet Bonanno's high standards. Ferri liked Tony because he worked hard and showed so much interest in everything going on. Tony, in turn, learned a great deal from his elderly supervisor and eventually dreamed of succeeding him when Gus retired.

Although most of the work force at Lionel was of Italian ancestry, with many men and women coming from overseas, the model shop was more diverse. To be sure, Gus Ferri had been born and trained as a machinist in Italy, as had Rocco Grieco, praised for his superb models. But five of the most talented model makers were German: Emil Albert, Rudy Hauptmann, Rudy Heller, August Juch, and Heinz Wiesener. Heinz, who died in 1995, remembered his peers as "good friends and true craftsmen." True, they endured a lot of ribbing, good-natured and otherwise, after the war. Yet all of them, Heinz added, enjoyed working at Lionel.

The work these experienced model makers did was uniformly outstanding. Most of their time was spent on an assortment of projects related to electric trains and accessories. Wiesener, for one, recalled the trials of making a preliminary model of the no. 132 Passenger Station. This item, the largest injection-molded piece planned by Lionel at the time of its introduction in 1949, taxed all of his expertise. Other modelers found themselves challenged to build models for Lionel's subsidiary lines, notably the Airex

Always fitting right in at Lionel, Tony (left) became a fixture on the Engineering Department's bowling teams during the 1950s and '60s.

fishing equipment and Linex camera. But nothing fazed them, Tony points out with admiration. Associating with the Germans left no doubt in his mind that their modeling techniques were well worth imitating.

His superiors grew fond of Tony. They chuckled at his brash manner and terrific sense of humor while appreciating his devotion to the craft of model making. Everyone made sure the kid was invited to the Christmas get-together in 1945. Amid the small talk and toasts, a gift-wrapped box appeared in front of Tony. "Even before I opened the box," he smiles, "Netta Pilecki and Viola Lombard [secretaries in the Engineering Department] had tears in their eyes. I tore off the wrapping and inside was a brand-new toolbox. I looked at the tools and began to cry, too."

CHANGE IN STATUS

Receiving the new toolbox intensified Tony's wish to become a model maker. That demanded training, which Ferri and Bonanno arranged. In 1946, Tony joined ten other fellows in Lionel's four-year apprentice program. Surprisingly, for someone who had never shown much enthusiasm for sitting in a classroom, Tony admits he enjoyed the geometry and drafting courses taught after his shift ended. But the on-the-job training was even better.

The first stop on Tony's journey through the factory was the Molding and Casting Department. Here, under the direction of Bill and Hugo Vezzozi, he studied metal die-casting as well as compression and injection molding. After the required two years, Tony was moved upstairs to the Tool Room, managed by Eddie Giaimo, whose brother Charles supervised the entire factory. Now approaching 19, Tony knew he still had plenty to learn, but the feeling of having to prove himself to everyone was gone.

During the next two years, Tony repaired tools and prepared drawings of machines and their components. Using those drawings, toolmakers produced the parts, then welded and machined them to put together finished items. Through these exercises, Tony improved his skills until at last Eddie Giaimo let him make his first die. Once it came out right, Tony began working with powdered metal, used to develop Magne-Traction.

With his apprenticeship behind him, Tony hoped to get back to the model shop. Fortunately for him, around 1950 or 1951, Gus Ferri had openings. The federal government had helped finance an addition to Lionel's plant where the defense projects awarded to the company would be designed and produced. Hearing Ferri's invitation, Tony never hesitated to return.

DEFENSE PROJECTS AND TRAINS

Once Tony was back in the model shop, he found himself in an odd position. He'd expected to work on electric trains. However, with the Korean War in full swing, Lionel received contracts to manufacture items for the armed forces. In fact, although few toy train enthusiasts know it, defense projects brought in needed revenue and launched notable research at Lionel throughout the 1950s. That Tony worked on these projects adds significance to his career there.

Tony was assigned to work with Patrick Tomaro Jr. on a government project involving bomb fuses. He enjoyed collaborating with the younger Tomaro, whose father ran the Machine Maintenance Department. Making the fuses more reliable and less expensive to produce challenged Tony. He didn't mind not working on trains, especially since he was overseeing a couple of younger model makers, Jack Powers and Louis Safonte.

More projects related to electric trains came Tony's way later in the 1950s. One that never made it to mass-production stands out. It's a version of the no. 3376 Bronx Zoo boxcar with poultry instead of giraffes. According to Tony, a tender was designed to hit a track trip and have a pair of chickens pop out on top of the pile of coal. Once a second trip was activated, a figure jumped up to catch the chickens. He never did, of course, and striking a third trip caused him and the poultry to disappear inside the tender.

Tony listened as one of the draftsmen described a new model.

Nothing came of this vanishing chicken car, although Tony claims it ran well and brought lots of laughs. The no. 3435 Traveling Aquarium car did make it into the Lionel catalog, and Tony was there when his buddy Anthony Rocco constructed a prototype. Later, Rocco used the same body shell for the 6445 Fort Knox Gold Reserve car. Was Lionel grateful? "Yeah," Tony scowls, "those cheap so-and-sos sent Tony Rocco a check for $200."

Tony had great respect for Gus Ferri, being honored at his retirement in 1956 by (left to right) Charles Giaimo, Joe Bonanno, and Philip Marfuggi.

Tony Gotto also played an active role in Lionel's race to capture part of the HO scale train market. Louis Safonte remembers the two of them modifying locomotives and rolling stock that Lionel had purchased. In addition, Tony may have helped with the 1957 catalogs by preparing prototypes of HO equipment for illustration. Photos he owns suggest that he took part in this project.

FROM LIONEL TO TOYS

Before retiring in February 1956, Gus Ferri discussed with Tony the possibility of his taking over the model shop. Tony remained optimistic, only to have his hopes shattered when Bonanno tabbed an outsider named Peter Nazar. For Tony, the reasons were obvious: Bonanno still thought of him as a kid and never forgot that Tony hadn't finished high school. Tony's skills as a model maker hardly mattered.

Disappointed, Tony let his friendships at Lionel, along with his participation on the bowling and golf teams there, sustain him. He still enjoyed working on trains and weapons; later, in the early 1960s, he joined another pal, Bernie Yuhl, in contributing to Lionel's science kits and slot cars.

By 1963, however, the situation at Lionel was deteriorating. To save money, the staff of the Engineering Department had been cut drastically. Joe Bonanno and Pat Tomaro Jr. resigned and were hastily hired by local toy makers. Meanwhile, Tony was having disagreements with the new chief engineer, Charles Montagna. Again he was in a situation of quit or be kicked out. As had been true in high school, Tony left, his pride intact.

His next stop was Deluxe Reading, a large toy manufacturer in nearby Elizabeth. Al Del Guercio, personnel manager at Lionel, mentioned that Bonanno was in charge of engineering at Deluxe Reading and might have an opening. Tony was hired, though not much time passed before Pat Tomaro Jr., now chief engineer at Remco, another toy firm, telephoned. He wanted Tony and

Heinz Wiesener remained friendly with Tony after leaving Lionel in 1956.

offered more money. Tony abruptly changed sides.

BELLEVILLE AND MOUNT CLEMENS

Throughout the postwar era, a number of the supervisors at Lionel started businesses to take advantage of the enormous demand for tooling and plastic parts. Members of the Engineering Department were part of this trend, either investing in small firms while remaining at Lionel or leaving to start their own. They dared to venture out on their own because working at Lionel enabled them to acquire the necessary knowledge, resources, and contacts.

Tony joined their ranks in 1964, when he established Donna Models, named after one of his daughters. He soon had more business than he could handle at his Belleville, New Jersey, molding shop, thanks to his links with Deluxe and Remco and the jobs Lionel cronies funneled his way.

Maintaining ties with Lionel proved valuable as General Mills struggled to assemble a new line of Lionel trains in 1969. Dick Brantsner depended on long-time employees still making and servicing trains at the factory. Lou Anzalone, Lenny Dean, Fritz Della Valle, and Jess Marchese, among others, shared what they knew. Brantsner turned to Tony and other workers to learn more.

Tony spent days and days at the Hillside plant. He patiently explained how trains had been produced and which tools and dies should be used. Everything was progressing until, much to Tony's disgust, Model Products Corporation (the division of General Mills handling electric trains) decided to shift production to its headquarters in Mount Clemens, Michigan.

The move made no sense to him; even so, Tony stayed in the game. He flew to Michigan every week for months to set up assembly lines and buy machines. Often when a fixture or die couldn't be located, Tony would fabricate one in his shop. Production went on, but the problems and inexperience were taking their toll. The low point for Tony came when he noticed the compressed-air presses weren't operating. He mentioned this to a foreman, who assumed the presses came with air packed in them! No wonder in 1971, Tony said "enough," and quit commuting.

COMING HOME

Back in New Jersey, life seemed very sweet. Old friends like Al Pascucci, Richie Rocco, and Nunzio Palumbo stopped by to shoot the breeze, and a

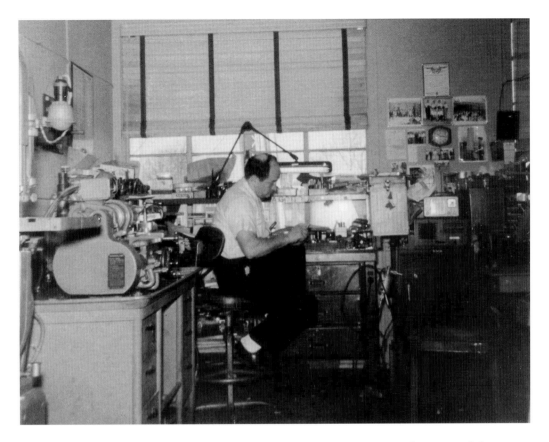

Surrounded by an array of machines and tools, Tony concentrated on one of the many projects assigned to him in 1961.

steady flow of orders reached Donna Models. Meanwhile, Tony had his hands full finishing the jobs while bringing his sons Anthony, James, and John into the business. Being so busy and knowing the production of electric trains no longer required his services, he could have put the past behind.

But turning his back on Lionel wasn't like Tony. Instead, he found a new way to show his appreciation to the supervisors who had trained him and the buddies he'd made at the factory. In the 1970s, Tony helped organize reunions involving dozens of former Lionel employees. Over dinner, salesmen, engineers, and assembly workers reminisced about the glory years, complained about how the company had shafted them, and razzed each other about hair lost and weight gained.

"The reunions were great," Tony says in a tone tinged with sadness as he remembers the friends who have died. Then he looks around his shop and realizes it stands as a testament to all he learned at Lionel. Tony Gotto keeps alive the heritage of that company as he and his sons mold items with care and precision. He shows that what was greatest about Lionel, even greater than the trains themselves, was the people who gave their all to make toys that will endure forever.

Photography and music are only two of the interests that Bill Vollheim has pursued during his life.*

BILL VOLLHEIM
Capturing Postwar Glories on Film

Advertising really took off at Lionel during the 1920s and '30s. The annual catalog seemed to grow larger and more attractive every year. Colorful illustrations of trains and accessories in national magazines caught the attention of kids across the country. Department store displays and radio promotions increased the public's awareness of new standard and O gauge models.

Credit for Lionel's triumphs in advertising likely belongs to several individuals, beginning with J. L. Cowen. Arthur Raphael also pioneered certain techniques that did much to bolster the popularity of Lionel's trains. Perhaps the key individual was Joseph Hanson, who served as advertising manager during the 1930s and for several years after the Second World War.

Hanson pushed hard to enhance Lionel's presence in various media, including Sunday newspapers and mass-circulation magazines. He wanted the trains to look exciting and attractive. That meant, on the one hand, using

---

* The color photographs in this chapter have not reproduced well because they are copies of the sole surviving prints, which were exposed to intense light over the past forty or so years.

illustrators to draw them in idealized settings and, on the other, having photographers show them in a realistic manner. Hanson did not hesitate to work with artists not on the company's payroll; they just had to be good.

Among the best of these outsiders was William Vollheim, a freelance photographer based not far from Lionel's headquarters. He became a favorite of Hanson's, and between 1948 and 1954 they worked together to promote electric trains in print and on television, and with a legendary model railroad. Bill remembers those days well and has many vivid memories to share

With such a hectic schedule at Diorama Studios, Bill needed time to relax, as he did here in 1949.

about the projects he worked on and the people he met at Lionel, including Cowen, who delighted in sharing jokes, homilies, and even a necktie with Bill.

LOOKING FOR WORK

Bill laughs when asked how much he knew about photography when he took a job at a studio not long after the war. "Not a thing," he admits, "but I was willing to learn." An eagerness to try something different and devote himself to it had characterized Bill's life from childhood into his early twenties. It enabled him to pick up knowledge from everyone he came in contact with and apply what he had learned to master novel situations.

Maybe you have to be that resourceful when you're an immigrant. Bill had come to America with his mother at age five in April 1928. He spoke only German, yet his parents expected to enroll him in public school less than six months later. Perhaps they worried about his progress, but their concern was unnecessary. Like so many young newcomers, Bill took to the streets of New York and grabbed what he needed. His chums taught him English—or at least a Brooklyn version of the language—not to mention many survival skills. Scarcely remembering the old country, he felt right at home here.

The Great Depression caused some hardship for the Vollheims. All the same, Bill thrived in elementary and high school, especially in classes where he was able to use his hands. He loved to tinker, and teachers applauded his talents. Yes, he did have Lionel trains to play with, although they didn't survive the rough treatment his younger brother gave them. "Too bad I don't have them," Bill says. Still, he doesn't seem to feel genuine regret that his brother put them through their paces so aggressively. Electric trains are designed for a kid's enjoyment, he realizes, even if that diminishes their value.

Joe Hanson, advertising manager at Lionel (standing left), often made use of Mac Ball Studios. Here, he confers with Mac (seated, second from left) on the composition of a photograph.

A few boring classes convinced Bill that college wasn't right for him. So in 1939 he hunted for work and soon was hired as an apprentice at Barach-Thurston Oxygen Equipment Co. in New York. Given this chance to learn a trade, he vowed to make the most of it. Within a year he was supervising the machine shop; by 1942 he had replaced his boss.

Bill couldn't help feeling restless, however, and was eager to try something else by the time peace returned in 1945. He had dabbled with photography as a hobby and wanted to improve his skills. The best way to master that field, he decided, was by learning from professionals, even if that meant starting at the bottom. Somehow he ended up knocking on the door of Mac Ball Studios, a small enterprise run by Mac and Murray Ball that was housed with dozens of similar businesses in Grand Central Palace, located at the corner of 48th Street and Lexington Avenue in downtown Manhattan.

Bill wanted a job, but confessed that he had no practical experience in photography. Such honesty as well as a desire to succeed impressed Mac. He hired Bill on the spot as a "go-fer." Grateful for the chance to learn, the young man never complained about the menial tasks he was told to perform or the low wages he earned. Soon he had graduated to the darkroom, where he developed the black-and-white preliminary prints Mac shot before taking the 8 x 10 color pictures that had built his reputation. "It was a beginning," Bill states, "and despite the long hours and hard work, I loved it."

"MEET MR. HANSON"

Not far from Mac Ball Studios, Joe Hanson and his small staff at Lionel were racking their brains to find novel ways of promoting Lionel trains. For all intents and purposes, though, the trains sold themselves in 1946 and 1947. Soldiers, sailors, and fliers were determined to enjoy all the benefits of civilian life denied them by economic depression and global war. Among the consumer items many craved were electric trains. They hardly needed reminders in

Lionel used only a handful of the photographs that Bill took of the dioramas Bob Sherman and he constructed in 1948. This one was published in the 1948 edition of Instructions for Assembling and Operating Lionel Trains.

magazines and newspapers that Lionel trains were exciting, enjoyable purchases. Still, Hanson felt driven to break into new areas.

Before and immediately after the war, Lionel had depended on color renderings to generate enthusiasm for its products. In catalog and commercial illustrations, artists exaggerated the size and detail of trains to boost sales. Hanson never abandoned this approach, but sought to augment it with photographs that generated enthusiasm in a different manner. Pictures, especially color ones, that depicted Lionel's trains and accessories in realistic settings could inspire boys and their parents to spend more money by showing them what they could do with those items.

That sales philosophy had influenced Hanson throughout his career. It had motivated him to launch *The Lionel Magazine,* which evolved into *Model Builder* in 1937. Even before the war officially ended, he had published *Candid Camera Shots—Lionel Trains in Action,* a pamphlet filled with photographs of O gauge trains in action on club layouts. In the year that followed, Joe supervised production of an additional brochure, *Plans and Blue Prints for Lionel Model Railroaders,* which offered tips to newcomers to the hobby. In the meantime, he offered help with *Model Builder,* pushing the notion that photographs should convey the fun and thrills created by building a layout.

Hanson's wish for more photographs led him to look beyond Lionel's advertising department for assistance. Toward the end of 1947, he approached Mac Ball about taking a series of 80 experimental color pictures of Lionel trains. Generally, when he did cast his net farther than 15 East 26th Street, the fish he went after were friends in related areas. In this instance, however, no evidence exists that he knew Mac. Maybe that's why he requested 4 x 5

Four of the other pictures Bill took of the first dioramas he built with Bob Sherman appeared in a 1949 display highlighting additions to the line.

color shots, although the Ball brothers specialized in 8 x 10s and probably did not own the equipment to shoot in a smaller format. The fact that Mac refused the job further suggests that he and Joe weren't acquainted.

Then Mac had an idea: Why not farm out the work to his lab assistant? He introduced Hanson to Bill, who fudged when asked about his experience shooting color photography. "I had none!" he confesses now, "but I wasn't about to let this golden opportunity pass by." Whether Joe was skeptical about the young man's abilities remains a mystery; even so, he gave Bill the job and told him to report to Lionel's headquarters. With Mac's blessing, Bill quit the studio and entered the ranks of free-lancers. Armed with a press-model Speed Graphic camera equipped with a Zeiss Tessar 135mm lens, he set off for his first major job, sometime in early 1948.

GETTING A PARTNER

On arriving at Lionel, Bill was told to take the elevator to the twelfth floor, where the Advertising Department was located. Once there, someone directed him to a room made of solid concrete for stability. That 15 x 20-foot room became his home away from home for more than half a year. There, Bill met Robert Sherman, the personable fellow who would be his partner in a host of projects over the next few years. The two hit it off immediately and made a superb team, one whose work left Hanson smiling with satisfaction.

Bob had been working at Lionel intermittently since 1938. He had done pen-and-ink drawings of O gauge equipment for newspaper advertisements and executed track plans prior to leaving Lionel during the war. Returning when the Advertising Department resumed its duties in 1945, he was kept busy sketching sets for the annual catalogs and constructing models and writing technical articles for *Model Builder*. But sitting by himself at a drawing table left Bob unfulfilled. So in 1947 he quit, determined to find a position that involved more interaction with people. Nothing developed, however, and

The last group of dioramas that Bob Sherman and Art Zirul built for Bill to photograph were larger and more elaborate than the earlier ones. This one featured the striking yellow and gray no. 2023 Union Pacific Alcos, new for Lionel's golden anniversary year of 1950.

within a week he had returned. A nervous Hanson, relieved to see Bob back, promised to ease his loneliness on the job.

The answer was to pair him with Vollheim. Their division of labor was obvious. Bob, an innovative and skilled modeler, designed dioramas featuring Lionel trains that Bill then photographed. They occupied most of their time building the scenes that Bob had conceived. As they cooperated, Bob taught Bill the secrets of the modeling trade. Before long they were turning out landscaped dioramas as quickly and cheaply as their boss desired.

Bill, meanwhile, was devising his own tricks for snapping pictures of the electric trains. He had to become as clever a magician as his partner. Sherman had experimented with illustrative techniques until he could make the images he drew appear authentic despite their not always conforming to reality. Playing around with linear perspective enabled him to depict Lionel's trains as larger than life; filling his sketches with details convinced viewers that what they were seeing was real rather than fanciful.

The challenge facing Bill was just the opposite. With his camera and lights, he had to create images that transcended reality in such a manner as to enhance the size and detail of their subjects. That meant devising methods of photographing Lionel's trains so that those in the foreground seemed bigger than they actually were. The answer was to shoot them from a low angle.

At the same time, however, Bill wanted to imitate Bob in improving the

Also new for 1950 were three items in this picture. In the foreground is a handsome no. 736 Berkshire and tender. The nos. 125 Whistle Shack and 456 Coal Ramp made their debut as well.

depth of field so that trains and accessories in the background were shown with clarity equal to those in the foreground. Like Sherman's catalog illustrations, Bill's pictures would offer observers more than a single point on which to concentrate and thereby capture more of their interest.

To accomplish his goal of creating an extremely wide depth of field, Bill moved in several directions simultaneously. First, to illuminate an entire diorama in the sharpest manner, he had to narrow the size of the aperture allowing light to reach the lens on his camera. He inserted a pinhole diaphragm holding a piece of brass into which he drilled a hole not much wider than a hair between the front and rear elements of the lens. Second, Bill bathed the scene with light generated by several photoflood bulbs situated less than a yard away. Third, after finally composing the shot, he experimented with long exposures, some lasting more than a couple of hours!

"I would set up the camera with a fixed tripod and trip the shutter," Bill recalls. Then he would lock the door of the studio and sneak off for a leisurely lunch with Bob. While they were gone, Bill's trusty Speed Graphic performed its magic. Sadly, few of the color pictures taken in 1948 were ever reproduced. Bill remembers handing sets of them to J. L. Cowen as well as the advertising staff. Why they elected not to use them baffles him. Neither does he have any clues as to what happened to the photographs. The trail went cold, and Bill's gorgeous depictions of Bob's dioramas were forgotten.

ONTO SOMETHING NEW

Bill scarcely had time to mourn his lost efforts, not when Hanson was beseeching him to help with a new project. During the summer of 1948, Hanson proposed that the American Broadcasting Company air a series of children's programs featuring Lionel trains. *Tales of the Red Caboose,* as this 13-week series was called, would open with Dan Magee, a retired locomotive engineer, dropping by the home of his neighbors, the Lane family. Young Larry Lane would turn to Dan for help with the layout he was building. As they worked, Dan would share stories of his years on the railroad, with the tales coming to life thanks to modeled scenes and stop-animation.

The amount of labor needed to construct the dioramas and handle the animated effects was staggering. There was no way Bill and Bob could do it independently, especially not when they had photographs and catalog illustrations to finish. Aware of this problem, Joe had approached a friend, George Schleining, for help in the spring. Schleining, who managed a small advertising agency in New York with Frank Hazell and already was involved with production of Lionel's catalogs, was offered a contract to oversee creation of layouts and animated sequences for *Tales of the Red Caboose.* To sweeten the deal, Hanson dangled additional work on the catalog, provided Hazell Schleining paid Sherman's salary.

Schleining and his partner took the bait. Why not? "Joe gave them $350,000 to $400,000 in contracts to produce the artwork," Bill points out. "That was important money in those days." Top priority in the summer of 1948 was the proposed television program. Hazell Schleining launched a separate firm to construct everything required to get *Tales of the Red Caboose* off the ground. Diorama Studios, as the new venture was named, hired Bill as manager. He recalls with humor its office at 128 West Fourth Street: "The property had been involved in a dispute after its owner died. So the heirs just split it down the middle. We rented one half, and the other was a nightclub called the Chantilly or the Pepper Pot. Unfortunately for us, the lavatories were in the other side!"

Sherman, Vollheim, and Arthur Zirul, just hired as a model maker, labored tirelessly on *Tales of the Red Caboose.* "We were young at the time," Bill chuckles, "and thrived on working around the clock." He isn't kidding, either. For each of the 15-minute episodes, they would get down to the dirty work on Monday, putting in a 12-hour day. "By Thursday, we'd be up until 2:00 in the morning," Bill continues, "because the film had to be at the studio on Friday to be broadcast that night at 7:30. Then we'd start over again the next day, tossing out ideas and planning what had to be built. It was 13 weeks of unbelievable effort, turning out about 2 minutes of film a day."

So much effort and so little to show for it. To the regret of Lionel enthusiasts,

Bob and Art filled this scene with freight cars and emphasized the grade crossing by which a no. 2344 New York Central F3 passes.

none of the episodes of *Tales of the Red Caboose* appears to have been preserved. Bill and Art, both of whom remember the filming as though it were yesterday, caution against getting too nostalgic about the series. "If you saw the programs now, you'd probably be disappointed," Bill states. He admits that the animated scenes were primitive by current standards. The figures were crude and hardly looked like people. Only the trains and the structures built by Art, Bob, and his friend Walter Hill distinguished the series. Still, hope lingers that kinescopes of *Tales of the Red Caboose* will surface.

THE MOST SPECTACULAR LAYOUT OF ALL

Demanding as making *Tales of the Red Caboose* turned out to be, it transformed Bill, Bob, and Art into an imaginative, industrious team. They liked and respected each other and knew they could collaborate to build outstanding models and smooth-running layouts. Their emerging sense of camaraderie couldn't have been better timed because, even before *Tales of the Red Caboose* ended in January of 1949, the fellows at Diorama Studies had turned their attention to another major project, one that would influence a generation of Lionel collectors and operators. It was the enormous O gauge model railroad built for the company's showroom in New York.

The driving force behind this monumental layout was Hanson. He was proud of all that his staff had accomplished, particularly Lionel's entry into television. Feeling confident about the future of trains, he convinced Joshua and Lawrence Cowen to underwrite construction of a new O gauge layout sometime during the autumn of 1948. If members of the Service and Display Departments got down to work in October or November, Hanson believed, they ought to have the model railroad up and running by the time the annual American Toy Fair took place the following March.

Of course, building a layout in the showroom wasn't anything novel. The presence of a large model railroad and a few small displays had been drawing visitors to Lionel's main office since the 1920s. In 1937, members of the Display Department had built an enormous layout to showcase the magnificent line of O gauge trains and accessories being introduced. This layout, which featured T-rail track and ample scenery, was refurbished immediately after the war. Miniature versions of Niagara Falls and the Grand Canyon, among other tourist spots, complemented the new trains on what became known as the Panorama layout. Three years later, Hanson was campaigning for a brand-new model railroad that would promote Lionel's product line for the second half of the century.

Not until November did the Service Department finish dismantling the old layout and start erecting plywood tables for the new one. The slow pace dismayed the Cowens, so a worried Hanson recruited Bill and his buddies to take over. They surveyed the situation and, with a burst of enthusiasm, made excellent progress following the plans that Sherman had sketched. Beginning in December, Art and Bob wired the track, accessories, and block controls. Steve Paganuzzi, another Diorama employee, made sure everything was operating flawlessly before they added scenery and structures.

No finer testimony to how much Bill had learned about building models existed than those he contributed to the showroom layout. Hanson hadn't intended for him to take an active role in the construction; better for Bill to concentrate on shooting pictures. As the schedule grew tighter, however, Joe changed his mind. "Help them out," he ordered Bill.

Laying down his camera, Bill rolled up his sleeves and assisted with laying the track. In his spare time, he built a few structures, one or two of which were based on projects that Frank Ellison, among the finest modelers of the period, originally designed for *Model Builder*. Bill recalls constructing the roundhouse and Ace Furniture Factory. Art goes farther and credits his friend with building the highly publicized J. L. C. Manufacturing Co.

With everyone at Diorama Studios pitching in, the layout came together right on time. "And everything worked like a charm," Bill says with a smile. "We included every accessory and operating car in the line: the milk car, the log loader, the magnetic crane, and the bascule bridge." Art adds that the Electronic Control Set ran without a hitch, as did Lionel's dapper GG1, thanks to an operating catenary system he painstakingly scratchbuilt. Toy buyers and distributors were dazzled from the moment they saw the fabulous layout.

This photograph, like some of the others Bill took in 1950, was reproduced in black and white the next year to illustrate Romance of Model Railroading with Lionel Trains. It contained an interesting mix of old and new items, with the heavyweight passenger cars cataloged for the last time in 1950 and the silver Alcos introduced in 1951.

Crowds of consumers felt the same. The New York showroom layout that Bill and his pals from Diorama constructed under incredible pressure became one of the most significant model railroads ever.

TROUBLE IN VIRGINIA, CALM IN NEW YORK

At last the Diorama crew could relax and catch their breath. Never again would the pace be quite so exhausting for them. Instead, they fell into a more normal routine that, while still demanding, was calm compared to what they had gone through between September 1948 and March 1949. Bill, Art, and Bob resumed their regular tasks of designing and constructing an array of small layouts. Some of these model railroads were destined to be used on television shows, including programs hosted by, among others, Jackie Gleason, Don Ameche and Frances Langford, and Kate Smith. Others were sent to the homes of celebrities like Gypsy Rose Lee and Arthur Godfrey, sometimes for their children and occasionally for themselves.

The temperamental Godfrey, feared by his staff and guests alike, proved to be a particularly tough customer. He insisted that Lionel provide his variety show with an elaborate layout each year around the holidays, and he never hid the fact that he intended to keep it. In 1953, he upped the ante and requested that Lionel install an entire layout in his home in northern Virginia. Hanson acquiesced and then passed the assignment to Diorama.

More than 40 years later, Bill and Art haven't forgotten anything about what they agree was an ordeal. Sherman, nominally a partner to Schleining since Hazell had left the agency, hastily designed an 8 x 16-foot layout for Godfrey. It took two weeks for Bill and his crew to finish construction. Next, they set out to transport the layout south and assemble it, all with only days to spare before Christmas. The problems encountered on that trip would have tried the patience of a saint. The truck broke down twice in New Jersey; then Bill realized he didn't have the address of Godfrey's estate. Obtaining directions from suspicious neighbors delayed him still more.

The troubles didn't end once the men reached the house. They found it impossible to carry the layout through the single tiny entrance to the basement where they were to install it. Bill had no choice but to cut in half each of the four 4 x 8-foot tables that comprised the model railroad and reconstruct them inside. His tired crew wrapped up the job around midnight, only to discover that a sudden snowstorm had left them stranded at the Godfrey home. Their ungrateful host provided next to nothing to eat and only the floor to sleep on. Needless to say, Bill recalls, "we couldn't wait to leave."

Life proved to be simpler away from the road. In the year or so after Diorama Studios built the showroom layout, Bill was paired with Bob on a project similar to their initial one. Throughout 1949 and 1950, they built elaborate dioramas to highlight such notable additions to the Lionel line as the Santa Fe and New York Central F3s, Union Pacific Alco diesels, nos. 681 Turbine and 736 Berkshire steam engines, and nos. 132 Passenger Station and 397 Operating Diesel-type Coal Loader. The beauty of these dioramas and the sharp images that survive leave no doubt that Bill and Bob made a terrific team.

These scenes have survived through sheer luck. Only a few pictures were published and then in black and white in *Romance of Model Railroading with Lionel Trains,* a brochure given away in 1951. Bill saved twelve of the photographs for his portfolio; eventually he put them on a lampshade. Years later, he was about to throw them away when a friend recommended keeping them. How fortunate that they can be enjoyed almost half a century after being shot.

LASTING LEGACY AT LIONEL

As important as the Diorama Studios photographs may be, they don't represent Bill's most lasting contribution to the Lionel story. During the early 1950s, he was instructed to take formal and candid shots of the New York

LIONEL

RAILROADING IS FUN!

LIONEL *ACCESSORIES GIVE IT REALISM*   *HOW TO BUILD REALISTIC SCENERY.*

Photographs that Bill took of the 1949 New York showroom layout appeared in a number of publications. This one illustrated the cover of an instructional poster available in 1951. Bill designed and built J. L. C. Manufacturing Co. in the center.

showroom. So many of the black-and-white images of the 1949 layout that appeared in popular magazines, especially *Toy Trains,* were taken by Bill. He captured the majesty of the unforgettable O gauge layout he helped construct in spectacular photographs that collectors treasure and study with care.

There are, for example, panoramic pictures that feature virtually all the layout as well as surrounding wall displays. These crisp photographs let viewers feel that they're standing in the Lionel showroom, waiting for sales personnel to return to their empty desks and describe new items in the line. Other photos focus on key scenes. Favorites include the bustling yard, with its turntable and roundhouse; the industrial area framed by nos. 97 Coal Elevator and 182 Magnetic Crane and the highway bridge; a corner containing the farm and footbridge Art built; and another corner with a subway line, railroad structures, and J. L. C. Manufacturing Co. Less familiar yet special in its own right is a picture Bill took with J. L. Cowen standing at the control panel.

Bill cherishes this last photograph because his friendship with Cowen still means a great deal to him. Although more than 50 years and a world of experiences separated the two when they met, they soon discovered how much they had in common. Lionel's founder enjoyed dropping in on his young friend as Bill composed the pictures he took of Bob's dioramas. They might compare notes on the special effects being created for Lionel trains or share thoughts on opera, religion, or politics. Cowen voiced opinions on just about everything, but he always liked to hear what Bill had to say because his views were the product of good judgment and common sense.

Managing Diorama Studios required Bill to walk over to Lionel and pick up the checks. Doing so afforded him opportunities to chat with J. L. Better yet for Bill, who was still in his twenties, he was able to learn from the elderly Cowen. "It never mattered how old J. L. was," Bill states, "He was a brilliant businessman. For instance, J. L. made sure never to sell quite as much as his customers wanted. He wasn't being unfair; instead, he was trying to keep the trains in demand and maintain his prices."

At the same time, Bill realized that Cowen was giving Lionel's customers more than they expected. He would hold back on the supply of electric trains, but do everything possible to provide excellent service. That's why, Bill points out, if an order left the factory short and a dealer complained, J. L. wouldn't blame whoever filled the order: "'We have good, competent people,' he would tell me. 'They don't make mistakes like that.'" Neither would Cowen doubt the dealer, who didn't want to pay for the entire order. On the contrary, "J. L. would always say, 'It's no big deal. Send it to him.' Don't question the dealer, and always keep good relations."

Cowen enjoyed a joke, especially if it conveyed a feeling that human nature is good and life is meant to be shared with others. Bill sensed that his boss had known difficult times, yet because he had succeeded and could enjoy the finer things in life, he carried no grudges and wanted to help others have as much fun. Cowen's generosity was unsurpassed, as Bill discovered the night he attended a party being given by J. L. Called aside, the photographer was handed a lovely necktie as a gift. "'I want you to have this Countess Mara tie,' J. L. told me. 'Think of me when you wear it.'"

LOOKING BACK WITH PLEASURE

The time Bill spent with Diorama Studios was filled with enjoyment. Even so, after five or six years he was feeling anxious, ready to move on and try something else. Perhaps the episode with Arthur Godfrey in late 1953 left him feeling burned out. Whatever the cause, Bill didn't shed many tears when, the following year, Lionel severed its ties with Diorama. Hanson had left the firm, and his successor didn't use the services of George Schleining's firm.

Bill departed in October of 1954, leaving behind Art and Bob. He eventually opened his own business, William H. Vollheim, Inc., where he cast models rather than photographing them. As you'd imagine, though, a camera has never been far from his hands. Memories of working at Lionel and the wonderful people he met there sustained Bill for many years. Even though J. L. Cowen, Joe Hanson, and Bob Sherman have passed away, Bill cherishes his experiences with them and values all they taught him. His photographs of the dioramas and showroom layout he helped construct make our memories of Lionel in the postwar era rich and vibrant.

Jack and Bea Kindler enjoy reminiscing about his years handling displays and promotions for Lionel.

JACK KINDLER

Goodwill Ambassador during the Postwar Era

"All of us who worked at the New York showroom enjoyed our jobs," states Bill Alpern, who worked there before and after the Second World War. "We had a great time demonstrating trains and relaxing after hours. Sure, going on the road could be exhausting, but we had such prestige being from Lionel. Of course, nobody had as much fun as Jack Kindler. No matter what the assignment, he had a ball."

Jack wouldn't deny a word of what his former colleague was saying. "Working at Lionel from 1946 to 1966 was a ball!" he smiles. "The people were terrific, and the trains were wonderful. I wouldn't trade those times for anything." One reason Jack had such a good time was his nature: He's a gregarious, sweet fellow. He likes to entertain others, whether by showing off examples of his sculpture or regaling them with stories of his days at Lionel.

Another reason Jack has many fond memories is that his job was special. Although based in New York, he wasn't a typical salesman, with an immense territory to cover and regular customers to visit. No, Jack was a demonstrator, which meant he usually could be found strolling through the showroom.

There, he kept an eye on the layouts and chewed the fat with members of the Service Department. Often he chatted with J. L. Cowen, interrupting their conversations to show brand-new models to kids off the street, local retailers, and major distributors.

Hanging around the showroom was just the beginning, however. Sometimes Jack accompanied salesmen on their tours. Alongside Joe Mariamson or Myles Walsh, he built department store displays and taught service station employees how to repair accessories. Nights were more carefree, and Jack sighs over the fine restaurants and splendid hotels he frequented. When not on the road, he fielded requests to design electric train displays and operate small layouts on television.

Soon after being hired Jack demonstrated the Electronic Control Set for George McManus (left), creator of the "Bringing Up Father" comic strip.

Jack's enthusiasm for coming to work was infectious. And why not? "Every day at Lionel was an adventure," laughs the firm's unofficial goodwill ambassador.

STANDING OUT WITH A SMILE

Jack could say that every day of his life had been an adventure up to the time he joined Lionel. His early years helped him develop a personality that was all but perfect for winning the trust of strangers and selling them toys. For Jack grew up on the road, where resourcefulness and an outgoing manner are vital to making friends. His father was part of a song-and-dance team that traveled the East Coast's vaudeville circuit. Jack, who was born in 1919, picked up jokes and a knack for making other people listen from a father whose livelihood depended on getting audiences to laugh and cheer.

In 1946, after five years in the military (both infantry and air force), Jack returned home to his wife, Bea, and their young daughter, Patricia. Now he faced the dilemma of finding a job and raising a family. Someone he knew passed along word that Lionel was hiring out-of-work actors to demonstrate trains during the holiday season. "It sounded okay to me," Jack remembers, "so I stopped by the showroom and filled out an application." By the time he got home, the phone was ringing. Larry Young, a senior salesman, greeted Jack with instructions to report the next morning.

Given a quick introduction to Lionel trains ("We couldn't afford them when

I was a kid," Jack declares), the young man was told to prepare for the onrush. Every day between Thanksgiving and Christmas, huge crowds of adults and children pushed into the compact showroom to admire wall displays and gawk at the newly refurbished O gauge model railroad in the middle. Feeling much as his father must have when on stage, Jack sized up the audience and made his debut.

Demonstrators were hired to operate the layout, so that's what Jack did. But always with a smile. People responded to his friendliness and listened as he recited what he had learned about the line. When Jack asked if he could help anyone, the words reflected

When Lionel made its debut on television in May of 1947, Jack and Frank Pettit (right foreground) made sure the demonstration layout ran well when Lawrence Cowen (rear left) operated the Electronic Control Set.

his sincerity. Then he stood back and fielded questions. To the best of his ability, he supplied answers or directed visitors to more experienced sales personnel. It was trial by fire, and a tired yet affable Jack came through fine. Though Lionel usually dismissed the demonstrators after Christmas, there was no doubt this one was going to stay.

"I was green," Jack admits, "and had lots to learn." He isn't talking about how to dress for his job or where to entertain clients. Rather, he needed to learn the ins and outs of the entire line, and fast! In 1946 and '47, that meant understanding how the Electronic Control Set operated, whether smoke pellets were toxic, what made the whistle blow, why the worm drive on the Berkshire improved its performance, and when the GG1 would be available.

Jack acquired a good part of his education by listening to Arthur Raphael as well as his very capable assistant, Sam Belser. Wisely, he also consulted Irving Shull, the acerbic supervisor of the Service Department. Shull dealt with salesmen in a wary fashion, giving no time to those cocky enough to think they knew everything already. From the start, however, he sensed that Jack was different, and they worked well together. Also impressed with the newcomer was Jimmy Santangelo, who ran the stockroom and also had little patience for most of the sales staff.

All of these gentlemen served as mentors for Jack. Raphael he remembers as "a beautiful, witty man. He liked me from the start." What else could the sharp-tongued national sales manager do with a guy who, when asked what his ambition was, shot back, "To have your job!" Jack speaks with even greater warmth and respect about Belser, "a sweet man, who took me under his wing and made sure my extra efforts were always rewarded."

Curiosity about how things worked proved to be a key ingredient in Jack's rise. "One day," he begins, "I kept hearing an odd noise from one of the locomotives on the layout. So I grabbed it and started taking it apart." No big deal, except that an alarmed J. L. Cowen spied Jack and burst out of his office, demanding to know what he was doing. "'Well,' I said calmly, 'if I'm going to work around here, I need to know more about the engines.' J. L. grinned, and from then on we were the best of buddies."

Knowing that Lionel's chairman liked him boosted Jack's confidence. "I had a pretty good idea they meant to hire me for the long haul," he smiles. "Larry Young, Myles Walsh, Joe Malcolm, and the other salesmen appreciated the kind of work I was doing for the people coming into the showroom. They told Ed Zier [Lionel's comptroller] that they needed me and I should not be let go." It was that simple. Once Jack was on the payroll, Raphael and Belser began scratching their heads as to how to use him.

The obvious answer was to assign Jack to a specific sales territory, but Raphael and Belser thought the new demonstrator had too much promise to be sent on the road. Instead, they wanted to capitalize on his artistic talents and growing knowledge of the line. So Jack continued to commute to 15 East 26th Street each day. There, he entertained visiting distributors and celebrities, not to mention tourists who might drop by without any warning.

For all of these visitors, Jack would, at the drop of a hat, put the trains on

Complete with an engineer's hat, Jack posed with this mock-up of a Lionel locomotive sometime in the late 1940s.

the central O gauge layout through their paces. Then, after displaying the company's best products, Jack often was asked to create a track plan for a small layout. He complied with ease, filling notebooks with simple sketches that he gave away by the dozens. Better yet, he made sure to specify how much track was necessary to build the individual layouts and to suggest appropriate accessories and transformers. If someone had a problem with a locomotive or operating piece, Jack usually could diagnose what was wrong. Lionel had indeed found a valuable player in its own backyard.

In 1957, Jack (left) designed a large layout for Wide, Wide World using Lionel's new line of HO scale trains.

GETTING "ZAPPED" BY J. L.

Among the men Jack worked with at Lionel, none meant as much as J. L. Cowen. They hit it off immediately. Jack's winning personality and fascination with the firm's products partially explain why Lionel's founder liked him. Just as important was Cowen's personality. Unlike so many self-made individuals, he never forgot his struggles to get ahead or ignored the people beneath him. Indeed, J. L. possessed that rare trait of relating well to men and women much younger than he. Sometimes that meant he pontificated and expected them to listen respectfully; more often, though, it involved "joshing" (pun intended) and waiting for them to give back as good as they got.

Jack neither feared nor worshipped J. L. The way he nonchalantly told Cowen why he was tinkering with a locomotive makes that clear. So does the exchange they had after Jack criticized a backdrop painted for a display layout. "'It's horrible,' I said to J. L. He bet me $100 that I couldn't improve it. 'You're on!' I replied. And I did it. Got the money without a word." Who can doubt that J. L. enjoyed paying every dollar to his "Jack of all trades"?

Lillian Cowen, whom J. L. married in November of 1948, recognized the rapport between the two men. "The first thing Josh does after waking up," she told Jack, "is figure out how he can 'zap' you." Jack said their bantering gave him a lot of pleasure, too. "J. L. challenged me, and I liked showing him how well I could master every task."

The second Mrs. Cowen (J. L.'s first wife had died in June of 1946) discovered how much her husband enjoyed "zapping" Jack not long after marrying. J. L. recruited Jack to drive them around the Thousand Islands region in northern New York for a two-week vacation. Once they pulled up at the home

By the mid-1950s, Jack was as much a fixture at the New York showroom as was the life-sized Pennsylvania Railroad Turbine steam locomotive display. Among his many responsibilities, Jack helped revise the brochures that Lionel offered retailers and set buyers.

of Victor Soskice, principal owner of Airex Corporation (a Lionel subsidiary that made fishing gear), Jack settled into a routine in which he spent days fishing with his boss and nights playing cards with both Cowens.

One day, J. L. slipped on a rock and hurt his back. Always the tease, he claimed that Jack had pushed him. In fact, he kept up the act for weeks, even complaining to irate factory personnel that he was the victim of Jack's bullying. An embarrassed Jack tried unsuccessfully to reveal the truth; watching him squirm pleased the playful Cowen.

Cowen visited the plant a few times each month, and he liked having Jack drive his Bentley to Hillside. On arriving, the "Old Man" turned into a tour guide, one who took pride in knowing the names of virtually everyone. With Jack marching behind, J. L. showed off his knowledge of various machines and then led him to the Engineering Department.

Once there, J. L. headed directly to the top-secret development laboratory. Like a kid snooping for Christmas gifts, he couldn't wait to find out what was happening there. One bellow was enough: Frank Pettit would come running to reveal what he was cooking up for next year's line. Next, Cowen usually escorted Jack through the rest of the department. He never missed checking up on the model makers and the technicians in the powdered metallurgy lab. When it was time for lunch, J. L. nudged Jack into the dining room used by such high officials as Charles Giaimo and Philip Marfuggi. "The food was excellent," Jack recalls, "and so was the wine."

Cowen became more talkative on the drive back to Manhattan. Jack vividly recalls him discussing the company and its products. "J. L. wasn't much on talking about sports or politics. Sometimes Larry [Cowen] came up in conversation. Overall, J. L. thought he was doing a good job as president.

He might question some of Larry's decisions, and I remember some arguments between them, but their devotion to each other was plain.

"Although J. L. didn't say much about Larry's divorce, I could tell the Old Man still liked the first wife's parents. Sometimes we drove by their home so J. L. could visit. Other times J. L. instructed me to pick up his grandchildren from his daughter [Isabel Brandeleone] and take them to a beach on Long Island to swim. The kids thought of me as just part of the family, and I guess that in some ways I really was."

EXPLOITS ON TV

The late 1940s were momentous times at Lionel. Among the most important changes occurring was a growing awareness that television could show the thrills and pleasures of playing with electric trains as never before. The benefits of putting Lionel's trains on this new medium weren't evident to J. L. or Lawrence Cowen. Even Joe Hanson, who often is credited with advocating for exposure on television, missed seeing the opportunities it offered. According to Jack, Bernard and Roz Relin, the brother-and-sister team spearheading Lionel's public relations campaign, saw first how much the firm could gain from having its products shown on different TV programs.

Lionel gained a foothold on television barely half a year after Jack was hired. In May of 1947, thanks to the Relins, Lawrence was a guest on an interview show broadcast in New York. He described Lionel's path-breaking Electronic Control Set to Harriet Van Horne, the host. Then they watched as the train was demonstrated. Handling the controls of a small layout was Jack, supervised by Frank Pettit. Although the trains were shown for only a few minutes, everyone involved agreed that the venture was worthwhile. For Jack, a new category on his résumé was about to be added.

Hanson, now convinced that television was essential to increasing sales, took a twofold approach to it. Jack's cooperation and expertise proved vital to both. One method was to have Lionel allot money and time to create series of its own. *Tales of the Red Caboose* (1948) and *Lionel Clubhouse* (1950) allowed the firm to concentrate on promoting trains in settings its employees controlled. Jack recalls helping with the first series but not the second. "On Fridays, while they were filming *Tales of the Red Caboose,* someone was needed to operate the layout. Guess who was asked? I was pleased and flattered by the assignment."

Once Hanson felt confident working with Jack, he followed a second, less expensive and labor-intensive course. Rather than having Lionel take responsibility for its own programs, he pushed for getting items on shows produced by networks and sponsored by national brands. For example, if a variety show featured a musical number related to railroads, Hanson suggested a Lionel layout be used with it. Producers liked that idea, and so, for only the cost of the trains, Lionel gained a wealth of publicity.

Other than a couple of people associated with Diorama Studios, the employee generally asked to supervise the use of Lionel's trains on television was Jack. He enjoyed watching the filming and running the trains. Meeting the performers was a pleasure, but Jack never became starstruck. His wife agrees: "Jack forgot most of the ones he met. He never noticed that one day John Wayne was having breakfast at the same table with him."

Among the prominent names Jack worked with in the early and mid-1950s, he mentions Jackie Gleason, Robert Q. Lewis, Ed Sullivan, Helen Hayes, and Hugh Downs. "Working with Gleason was a treat," he says. "One time I put a shot glass on a flatcar, and he

During the filming of Christmas in the Park, a television special, Jack (center right) and advertising manager Jacques Zuccaire (left) worked closely with Harpo Marx.

yells on camera, 'Booze goes great with Lionel trains!' I thought J. L. would have a fit!" Another time, Art Carney asked Jack to hold two chimpanzees behind the curtains for a planned skit. "Out of nowhere, one of them bit me on the tail. I screamed in pain, and Art was hysterical with laughter!"

Not quite as zany yet about as unpredictable was Dave Garroway. Jack recalls appearing with him in 1957 on a show called *Wide, Wide World*. "What was great about that was that I brought my son along, and Kenny was shown with me. Boy, did that make him a hero in the neighborhood! Garroway was relaxed and sure liked the trains. He wanted tracks laid all over the studio. Once the cameras were rolling, he told me to run the trains everywhere. You could tell he was having a terrific time."

Surprisingly, Garroway didn't imitate other TV stars by insisting that Jack design a layout for him or let him take home the Lionel equipment. Not everyone was so accommodating. After they became acquainted, Jackie Gleason kept Jack hopping by asking question after question about electric trains and then demanding that he stop by and tune up the star's home layout.

Jack rarely balked at the extra work. "When I started at Lionel I was paid $35 a week. Anything I could do to supplement that was great, including building layouts for people who stopped by the showroom or I met through TV: Frank Sinatra, Roy Campanella [catcher for the Brooklyn Dodgers], Walter Chrysler, Freddie Fields [producer of Broadway plays], and Tommy Manville, a rich playboy. They heard what I did, and the next thing I knew a limousine was picking me up so I could build or fix up a layout for them."

Fortunately for Jack and his family, most of his rich and famous patrons expressed gratitude for his efforts. He was paid nicely and thanked profusely.

Sometimes flowers were sent to his home, while on other occasions toys were delivered to his three children. "Roy Campanella owned a liquor store in Harlem, so he sent over bottles of his favorite brands. Freddie Fields knew a designer of children's clothes, so my daughter received dresses."

Few of the celebrities Jack encountered displayed an air of superiority. First of all, they appreciated his work and recognized that, as Bea puts it, "He knew something that they didn't." More telling, the movie stars, professional athletes, and heirs to fortunes shared with Jack a love of Lionel trains. "There was a genuine sense of camaraderie among us," he states. "Electric trains leveled people. They came to the showroom and loved what we had. And we loved what we had. Lionel was an open door, and we all walked through it."

Lionel produced a number of commercials in 1962 to promote its space and military trains. As usual, Jack supervised the project.

BIGGER AND BETTER ASSIGNMENTS

By the mid-1950s, Jack occupied an influential position at Lionel. Executives from the Cowens down paid attention to his suggestions on developing the line and promoting new items. Salesmen, from 30-year veterans like Larry Young to recent additions like Ronald Saypol, trusted him to keep them abreast of what was happening at the plant and in the field. They listened when Jack recommended an item to push or argued in favor of a display. As an indication of how much Lionel depended on him to streamline its sales pitch, he was told to refine *Know the Answers and Sell More,* a brochure for retailers, and to revise *How to Operate Lionel Trains and Accessories,* an instruction booklet for first-time buyers.

Given Jack's penchant for designing layouts, it isn't surprising that he started campaigning for a new O gauge model railroad at the New York showroom in 1954 or '55. He practically lived there and knew every nook and cranny of the current layout. Improving sections of that model railroad was only a stop-gap measure, he told J. L. The time had come to tear it down and construct a better layout.

Cowen, accustomed to Jack's drive, knew better than to ignore his chief demonstrator and layout designer. "If you can come up with something better," he needled Jack, "go ahead and prove it!" Feeling challenged, Jack whipped out a pencil and paper and began drawing. One advantage was that he knew Lionel intended to introduce a realistic system of O gauge track. "We had talked about it at a sales meeting," he recalls. "Everyone had liked the track, but we were stumped on what to name it. J. L. and Larry proposed Super O, which wasn't spectacular, but did the trick." Now Jack wanted to incorporate the new track, with its thin, darkened center rail and ample wood ties, into the layout he was designing.

Work began in the fall of 1956. "J. L. gave me freedom to do what I wanted," Jack remarks. "All I had to do was give instructions to Carmine Quatraro and the other carpenters from the factory." Also helping were Joe Donato Jr. and a few of his men from the Display Department, along with Irving Shull and anyone on his staff with idle time. Cooperation led to excellent progress over the winter. A few structures from the 1949 layout were installed on the new one; otherwise, it differed from its predecessor.

"Carmine was great to work with," Jack says. "What a craftsman! He built the control booth overlooking the layout. The booth was my idea, and I think it added a lot of excitement. We would laugh about J. L.'s wanting to interfere. Carmine said he was going to put up some extra lights in the ceiling to give J. L. something to worry about so he wouldn't bother us. By the time the layout was finished, just in time for Toy Fair in 1957, J. L. and Larry were very happy with it. So were Alan Ginsburg [who became executive vice-president after Raphael's death in 1952] and Jacques Zuccaire [who became advertising manager after Hanson left in 1954]. J. L. awarded me a beautiful watch, not to mention my usual $1,000 annual raise."

Jack had no time to stop and congratulate himself. He was too busy putting together promotional ideas and working with the Premium Division to come up with "tie-ins" and "bounce-backs." For example, he helped with a series of cardboard cutouts of Lionel locomotives and motorized units printed on the inserts in Nabisco Shredded Wheat cereal in 1957. Producers of children's TV shows requested Lionel layouts, and Jack felt compelled to dream up something outstanding for each of them. He also labored on the enormous layouts that went on display at Grand Central Station and Pennsylvania Station in Manhattan to raise money for the Fresh Air Fund every year. And he coordinated with Bachmann Bros.' efforts to market a number of that firm's Plasticville structure kits as parts of Lionel's O and HO gauge lines.

The range and number of projects involving Jack just seemed to multiply the longer he was at Lionel. Why, he even contributed to the product line by visiting metropolitan rail yards to see the latest equipment on real railroads. One day he caught sight of a handsome green car used to carry mail and packages by the Railway Express Agency. Suitably impressed, Jack proposed at an executive meeting that Lionel offer an O gauge model of this new car. Told to proceed, he quickly obtained plans and financial backing from REA so Lionel could eventually bring out the no. 6572 Railway Express Agency refrigerator car (first cataloged in 1958).

Putting in long hours to promote the line, Jack scarcely noticed that changes were taking place at the company. J. L., nearly eighty years old, spent less time in New York and had little to say about day-to-day affairs. Meanwhile, sales continued to decline and major stockholders fretted as their dividends grew smaller. Without warning in late 1959, J. L. sold his shares to Roy Cohn and cut Larry adrift. Such a dramatic change at the helm left employees reeling. Jack couldn't avoid feeling uneasy about his prospects.

MAKING THE BEST OF THE '60S

The first year of Roy Cohn's regime must have been troubling for Jack. Several supervisors at the factory were forced out, which weakened morale there. In New York, old-timers like Sam Belser felt pressured to leave. Sad to see one of his mentors treated badly, Jack wondered what was going to happen to friends closer to his age, who had joined the firm after the war.

Somehow, through hard work and a fair amount of luck, Jack and buddies like Myles Walsh, Bill Gaston, and Jerry Lamb held on. So did Malcolm and Mariamson, fellows whose ties with Lionel stretched back to the prewar era. Once Jack felt his position was secure, he set about making himself indispensable to Cohn and John Medaris, the new president. As was true when the Cowens ran Lionel, the array of talents he marshaled and the many links he had forged throughout the toy business combined with his reputation for honesty and industry to keep him safe.

To be sure, Jack didn't agree with everything Cohn did. In retrospect, he believes that diversifying the toy line by acquiring Porter Chemical Co. made sense, but allocating resources to develop a series of science kits did not. Broadening the O gauge line with military-oriented operating cars and accessories gets Jack's grudging approval; designing smaller versions of those items to bolster the already weak HO line does not. Buying electronics and aeronautical producers in hopes of transforming Lionel into a force in the space industry strikes Jack as an effort that was doomed to failure. "We all sensed that the company was in decline," he says. "The question was whether it could survive and keep us employed."

Still, Jack wasn't content with simply holding on. He was too busy assisting an enthusiastic bunch of public relations staffers eager to plug a variety of new products. One day he might show up at the Bronx Zoo to unveil the entertaining no. 3376 car with its bobbing giraffe. The next, Jack could be photographed with a budding starlet as he explained Lionel's military instruments. On another, he might spend hours conferring with George Marko about an elaborate display layout Marko was going to supervise for an international trade show in Russia. The assignments challenged Jack and renewed his hope that the company could thrive despite the changing market.

Arranging many of these promotional opportunities was a young woman hired by Tex McCrary Associates, an advertising firm that Cohn liked to use. Although Lionel was a client of hers for less than a year and soon after she would transfer her skills to television, Barbara Walters left an impression on Jack for her dedication and imagination. According to him, this future celebrity was "vibrant and very capable. You knew she was destined for greater things than PR work for Lionel."

One of Walters's major projects at Lionel was a television special broadcast toward the end of 1961. *Christmas in the Park* featured the new trains, science kits, and chemistry sets on display and in action in settings around New York's Central Park. Actors well-known, soon-to-be-known, and totally unknown shared the stage with the toys. An aging and tired Harpo Marx came to life as he joined Jack in operating a layout. Carol Burnett, just making a name for herself in show business, touted chemistry

The Fresh Air Fund received Lionel's support for many years. In 1963, Jack designed this layout for the well-known charity, helped install it in Grand Central Terminal, and then posed at the opening with singer Kaye Ballard (right) and terminal manager S. T. Keiley (center).

outfits. Once more, Lionel and Mr. Kindler found themselves in prime time.

Television specials and photographs in *Life* magazine showing hundreds of tiny Lionel submarines on the attack at Weekee Wachee Springs, Florida, more than pleased Jack's new bosses. Cohn invited his "Special Presentations Director" (Jack's ultimate title) to accompany the staff to the Stork Club. Smiles faded, however, when top executives realized that sales were falling short. Frightened though they might be, most members of the New York staff couldn't imagine Lionel collapsing. The smart ones, including Jack, began looking around and talking with friends in the business.

For years, he had maintained close ties with Jack Marion, the owner of Industrial Display Inc., a firm that had been constructing displays for Lionel since the early 1950s. Marion recognized that Jack would be an asset to his company and dropped hints that, should he leave Lionel, there would be plenty of jobs to keep him busy.

Robert Keeshan also expressed a willingness to help. Known to the world as Captain Kangaroo, Keeshan had met Jack in the early 1960s, when he first asked Lionel to exhibit new and antique electric trains on his morning show. His request had been directed to Jack, who had responded with speed. "I often heard from the Captain Kangaroo staff for assistance with props or railroad stories. So I would call my friend Lou Shur, who ran Madison Hardware, to see if we could borrow a few standard gauge and ancient O gauge pieces." Jack goes on, "Lou and I had been friends for a long time. He and his wife would entertain our whole family at their home on Long Island almost every summer."

Optimistic that Marion could steer work his way, Jack handed in his resignation at Lionel in 1966. He left reluctantly because he had spent so many rewarding years there and made dozens of friends. Yet he had observed so much that indicated the company might never recover from its downward spiral. The magnificent Super O layout he had designed and helped build in 1957 was gone six years later. Jack had supervised its dis-

With his good friend Al Gasparini (left), Jack explains the features of one of Lionel's science kits to the host of a television show in New Haven.

mantling as the famous showroom at 15 East 26th Street was shut down. No one at the helm seemed to know what direction Lionel should take, particularly not after the tyrannical Robert Wolfe assumed control in 1964. "Better to leave now," Jack realized, "while I have options and many positive memories."

ON TO MORE REWARDING TIMES

Jack was one former employee who proves there was life after Lionel. Handling a variety of projects for Industrial Display kept money rolling in for the Kindlers. Things weren't always great for them, but Jack never looked back. Then, with Marion's aid, he heard about an opening at American Telephone & Telegraph that involved performing promotional work similar to what he had excelled at during his tenure at Lionel. The rest was easy, just a matter of applying and waiting to be taken on as a field consultant.

Beginning in 1966, Jack free-lanced tirelessly for AT&T. His 20 years there matched his stay at Lionel. The work was enjoyable, but Jack had no regrets about retiring when he reached his mid-sixties. Since leaving he has been content to paint and sculpt, travel with Bea, and play with their grandchildren. Life has been good to Jack, and he has many wonderful memories of Lionel to share, along with stories of his father's career. Like J. L. Cowen, Jack Kindler has been able to find the best in the people he's met and have fun working with them. We should all be so lucky.

George Vitt has long been interested in science and electronics.

GEORGE VITT

Exploring New Fields in Electronics

If asked to describe The Lionel Corporation, nearly all of us would respond, "An electric train manufacturer." Told to expand on this, we might recall that Lionel also marketed Airex fishing equipment and Porter chemistry sets and refer to it as a "toy and sporting goods maker."

These answers make sense, yet as the experiences of George Vitt make clear, they're too narrow. While at Lionel, he contributed to a range of products, including military instruments, a stereo camera, and an artificial hand. All demonstrated how innovative this firm was in using electricity to improve life.

George emphasizes that Lionel was a pioneer in applied research and development. He applauds the work done by the Engineering Department under Joseph Bonanno and the Electronics Laboratory under John Salles and John DiGirolamo. George's part in the Lionel story helps us appreciate its trains and understand why they were designed and built with care and durability.

REVOLUTIONS, WAR, AND FISHING

By the time 24-year-old George Vitt Jr. accepted a job at Lionel in 1949, he'd experienced more adventure in his life than most of his peers. His family's story begins in Czarist Russia, where one of his grandfathers served as minister of finance to Nicholas II. The other amassed a fortune in the fur and match businesses estimated to have been in the millions of rubles. Such circumstances would have guaranteed George a life of ease had the Russian government not been brought down during the revolution of 1917. When it crashed, virtually all the family's wealth disappeared. Somehow, they escaped the blood-letting and made their way to America.

Not long after George's parents became citizens of the United States, they again found themselves abroad. His father, a mining engineer employed by Caterpillar Tractor Co., was dispatched

George contributed to a variety of projects while working in the Engineering Department at Lionel from 1949 to 1956.

to China and Japan, where he served as sales manager. George arrived in 1925: "I was conceived during a family visit to Stockton, California, and born in our home in Manchuria."

Growing up in Asia, young George attended private schools. He studied hard, took up sports, and learned to beware of kidnappers and drug smugglers. His lifelong fascination with Oriental art and weaponry, not to mention photography, dates from these years.

Life became even more precarious after Japan conquered Manchuria in 1931. Abductions and shootings increased because some local merchants aided the invaders. The Vitt family returned permanently to the United States in 1935. Eight years later, George enrolled in the Massachusetts Institute of Technology. Then, in 1944, he enlisted in the navy, along with most of his fraternity brothers. The navy trained him to be a radio technician and shipped him to the Philippines. There he taught classes and explored the islands.

George returned to MIT after the war, no longer terrified by electrical engineering. In the meantime, his father, an avid fisherman, had taken a job with Ocean City Manufacturing Co., a Pennsylvania firm that sold fishing equipment. Sometime toward the end of 1948, Vitt Sr. was approached by Lionel. As Arthur Raphael explained, Lionel had purchased control of Airex Corporation, a maker of fishing reels. The smooth-talking Raphael hoped to lure Vitt aboard as sales manager at Airex.

Problems erupted soon thereafter, however. Vitt didn't get along with Victor Soskice, who supervised the Airex operation. Also a refugee from Russia, Soskice had yet to pick up an egalitarian touch. He treated his staff with disdain. Before long, Vitt was looking for a way out, which he wrangled from Lionel at the end of 1949.

During his brief association with Lionel, Vitt inquired about a job for his son. Privately, he told Joseph Bonanno to hire George Jr. and teach him everything about industrial engineering from the bottom up, his first task to be

Perhaps George's most important project relating to electric trains was the development of Magne-Traction, as announced in Lionel's catalog for 1950.

"sweeping the shop floor." Bonanno agreed to interview the young man and came away suitably impressed. He wisely ignored the father's recommendation about that initial assignment.

George approached the job eagerly. True, he'd never given Lionel any thought while at MIT. Yet as a recent graduate, and a newly married one at that, he felt lucky to have a job, even if it paid only $37.50 a week. Besides, he didn't expect to spend his entire career at Lionel. George dreamed of gaining valuable experience and perhaps enjoying a little more adventure while making toy trains.

A KIND OF MAGNETISM

Almost from the day he arrived, George found himself immersed in advanced research projects that involved diverse materials, theories, and processes. And that was just fine with him.

"Lionel," he says, "provided a fantastic introduction to engineering because you could exercise all the talents you had." Bonanno encouraged his staff to conduct research that would help develop new items, reconfigure individual parts, or improve production techniques. To assist engineers in discovering the practical aspects of their analyses, he gave them access to presses, lathes, and milling and die-cutting machines. There was also a well-equipped electronics laboratory. "No better arrangement could be imagined."

Young engineers flourished under Bonanno's system. So did the chief engineer. Before George's arrival, Bonanno had contributed to the development of a smoking locomotive and a simulated diesel horn. His most ambitious project was an electric train operated by radio waves. He translated this vision into reality with the 4109WS Electronic Control Set, which was cataloged for the first time in 1946. The locomotive's direction and whistle, along with the car couplers, were controlled by miniature radio receivers installed in the tender, and each freight car operated by radio waves transmitted through the rails. The transmitter had multi-frequency capability.

George played a key role in one of his boss's most important achievements, one that enabled locomotives to stay on track better while increasing their pulling power. Bonanno had taken an interest in the new field of powdered metallurgy, curious as to how magnetic materials could im-

In 1951 or '52, someone caught George deep in thought at his desk.

prove Lionel trains. Experiments were under way when Vitt joined the department. Bonanno assigned him to work with George Jurasov on the secret program that culminated with the introduction of Magne-Traction in 1949.

The idea behind Magne-Traction was simple. How much a locomotive could pull (drawbar pull) was related to the friction created between its wheels and the track when power was delivered to it. The more a locomotive weighed, the greater the friction. Of course, the more it weighed, the more power that was needed to move it and any cars coupled to it, especially up a grade. So Bonanno was looking for a way to raise drawbar pull without increasing weight.

Permanent magnets offered an answer. Attaching small Alnico Vl magnets inside a locomotive, adjacent to the drive wheels, would strengthen its hold on the track without adding significantly to its weight. More friction would result, enabling the locomotive to pull more rolling stock. However, the die-cast wheels used at that time would have to be replaced by ones made of ferromagnetic material.

Bonanno's knowledge of powdered metallurgy convinced him that Lionel could mass-produce sintered-iron wheels. Through experimentation, Jurasov and Vitt learned how to compress, heat, and bind powdered metal to form rugged yet smooth wheels and rollers that didn't require finishing. These parts bolstered the magnetism of each engine, thus increasing its drawbar pull. The oil impregnation originally used on the sintered-iron wheels to prevent rust had to be modified because of its great reduction of friction.

Determining the ideal alloy material, shape, and position of these magnets was critical. George studied the wheel geometry of different Lionel engines to learn where to fit the tiny rectangular and cylindrical magnets that were made to Lionel's specifications by Crucible Steel Co. and Indiana Steel Products Co. He also designed the needed magnetizer and magnetic measurements

106

Associates in the Engineering Department celebrated the holidays together. George snapped this picture at one gathering (clockwise from the left): Morris Zion, John DiGirolamo, Elizabeth Bonanno, Joseph Bonanno, Bill Jefferies, Jeanne Vitt, Henrietta Salles, and John Salles.

instrumentation and ran innumerable tests to determine the relative strengths of these various magnets.

From a single locomotive equipped with Magne-Traction in 1949 (the no. 622 NW2 switcher and its O27 twin, the no. 6220), Lionel went to a full line of new and more powerful O gauge engines the next year. Modelers were pleased and praised this key breakthrough. Bonanno had achieved another triumph, thanks to the diligent, innovative work done by Jurasov and Vitt. For George, the tedious experiments had paid off handsomely in greater respect and responsibility at Lionel.

NEW FRIENDS AND WEAPONS

Always interested in what was going on around him, George was quick to ask questions and make friends. Even the model makers, often a crusty and suspicious group, came to trust him, because of his humor and intelligence. George shared his ideas with them and turned to them for advice on how to operate different machines. He laughed at their jokes and the pranks they played on each other.

A favorite story of his recalls the time Rudy Hauptmann was lighting an acetylene torch at the rear of the model shop. "He had a 24"-long yellow flame going when someone called to him. Not thinking, Rudy turned to see who it was. The flame hit one of the sprinklers on the ceiling! Suddenly there was water everywhere! The entire shop was flooded!"

On drier days, Bonanno and his chief assistants, Morris Zion, John DiGirolamo, and John Salles, had time to observe George's talents. They liked his easygoing personality and commented on his reliability. He'd do well, they believed, regardless of how long he chose to stay at Lionel.

Salles, who was in charge of the Electronics Laboratory when George arrived at Lionel, became one of George's closest friends. They shared a love of outdoor sports, particularly skin diving and canoeing. With their wives, they took vacations together, hiking and camping in New Jersey and Delaware and going on a memorable trip to the Florida Keys, where they tested a pneumatic spear gun developed by Salles's brother in France.

George was ready with his camera when members of the Engineering Department presented Joe Bonanno with a pen-and-pencil set in December of 1952.

Whether swapping war stories or collaborating on engineering projects, Salles was always good company because of his terrific sense of humor. "I'll never forget how John made us laugh when Jerry Ritchelli and I were doing preliminary work on a talking station," George begins. "We asked John to pretend he was a station master announcing trains arriving and departing. We'd roar listening to John repeat endlessly, 'All aboard! All aboard!' in his thick French accent. Can you imagine the looks on the faces of kids and their parents if they'd bought a toy with sounds like that?"

More serious work with Salles began in 1951. With the Korean War spreading, several government agencies awarded military contracts to Lionel. George's familiarity with acoustics benefited the company as Lionel tackled projects involving sound and ultrasonics.

The U. S. Signal Corps at nearby Fort Monmouth wanted Lionel to improve the headsets soldiers in tanks used to communicate with one another. As George explains, this entailed modifying both the speaking and the listening devices. He and his assistants had to devise a microphone that could minimize the surrounding noise when someone spoke into it and earphones that eliminated much of the ambient noise that interfered with the messages.

George designed all the necessary acoustic testing apparatus, which used soundproof chambers, sweep generators, logarithmic recorders, oscilloscopes, and calibrated condenser microphones from Western Electric and Altec-Lansing. After months of difficult, often frustrating effort, he announced he'd come up with novel designs that met the tough specs. He depended on a carbon microphone to "cancel" various noises, while using a tube that went directly from the new earphone into a soldier's ear canal.

George's innovations met frequency-response criteria as well

George served as president of the Professional and Technical Workers Union for three years while at Lionel. Assisting him were (left to right): Joseph Festa, Abe Kagan, and Charles Montagna.

as sensitivity standards. The improved headsets were more effective and less expensive to produce than older ones, which greatly pleased the military. Resulting contracts for large-scale production as well as new headset designs proved to be quite profitable for Lionel.

"The headset was a perfect project for Lionel," observes George. "It was a small, precision electrical assembly, and we were used to handling that kind of device. Also, Lionel had production lines where people knew what to do and how to test the end-product." In short, manufacturing electric trains had taught Lionel's engineers, machinists, and assembly-line laborers skills that were put to good use with other projects during the postwar decades.

For that reason, George concludes, Lionel should not be perceived as simply a maker of toys. Because its trains were powered by small electrical motors produced in its own factory, Lionel was more of a manufacturer of precision electromechanical assemblies and appliances.

Yet, George adds, "even that description isn't adequate. Bear in mind that Lionel was a pioneer in materials research involving various plastics and powdered metallurgy. It was producing sophisticated and precise instruments for the armed forces, virtually entirely with subassemblies made in-house. Lionel was a rare example of a firm engaged in all kinds of research for which its employees were expected to find applications."

This expansive, forward-looking vision of the company emerged not from corporate headquarters in Manhattan but from the factory in Hillside. "Joshua and Lawrence Cowen didn't foster this view," George asserts. "Joe Bonanno did. He was the captain of the ship at Lionel. He wouldn't get his hands dirty the way the rest of us would, especially Salles. Joe would come up with the ideas, and in many cases it was up to us to invent and make them work. But what incredible ideas they were!"

WATCHING THE BIRDIE

Life at Lionel wasn't all work. There were wonderful opportunities to play and George took advantage of them. His memories begin with food, as buddies shared Italian dishes. His mouth waters as he thinks of the chicken cacciatore one restaurant simmered for 24 hours to Nat Donato's specifications. On another evening, after attending a lecture, Joe Bonanno treated George and other engineers to dinner at a Greenwich Village *trattoria* where the mussels and escargot "were without peer."

Production workers at Lionel tested the headset that George helped develop for the U. S. Signal Corps during the Korean War.

Even the artificial food at Lionel wasn't bad! "Larry Cowen had hired a chemist named Mort Gallison to perform some odd jobs," George relates, "including the development of synthetic smells. One of these was frying bacon! For weeks a section of the Engineering Department smelled like a hamburger joint. I still don't know whether Mort's experiments were successful or what Larry had in mind when he gave out the assignment, but the odors were fantastic! Joe Sanford, who was designing Lionel's stereo camera, shared an office with Mort and gave us a smell-by-smell account."

Food and drink call to mind the holiday parties that were thrown by departments at the Lionel factory. Draftsmen, designers, model makers, and others relaxed with their spouses, enjoying champagne fountains, platters heaped high with food, and swing music provided by Breezy Smith, a local band leader who toiled on Lionel's assembly line during the week.

As George watched everyone laughing and dancing, he felt the urge to snap some photographs. No one minded when he showed up with a camera, and they smiled on command and continued to enjoy themselves. George built his own strobe flash, using parts given him by Dr. Harold Edgerton of MIT, inventor of the strobe. Without this device, George could not have captured all the fast-action scenes. Today, the dozens of pictures he took keep alive the image of Lionel as family, a place where relatives worked and lifelong friendships were forged.

HANDING OVER THE CREDIT

One man George occasionally caught with his camera was Charles Giaimo. No one at Lionel after the war could miss him. For one thing, he held the position of works manager, which meant he supervised all operations at the factory. For another, nearly everyone there revered the congenial Giaimo as a hero.

Most employees knew how, through grit and ingenuity, he'd risen from toolmaker's apprentice in 1917 all the way to Lionel's board of directors. Then in 1937, tragedy struck. Giaimo contracted multiple sclerosis. But he'd refused to surrender to the disease, fighting to hold on to his job and maintain a normal life. By the time George Vitt was hired, Giaimo was a familiar sight maneuvering along assembly lines in an electric golf cart.

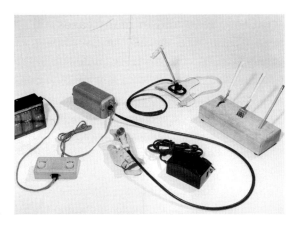

Developing an electric hand and its accessories for a young man injured in an automobile accident meant a lot to George.

The two men had little formal contact until a horrible car accident in 1952 drew them together. Giaimo heard that the son of his physician, Dr. Richard Brickner, had been badly hurt. One day the boy was musing about his acceptance to Harvard University and the next he faced the prospect of being paralyzed for life. His father turned to Giaimo, who pledged to find a way to alleviate the boy's helplessness. Giaimo conferred with Bonanno, whose faith in George's abilities convinced him the young engineer could help. A meeting was called, and work began.

George came up with several ideas that incorporated gadgets developed for Lionel's trains. Six months of trial and error produced a remarkable "electric hand." The device, which used the motor from a no. 364 Conveyor Log Loader, the E-unit from a no. 2343 F3 diesel locomotive, and the drag mechanism from an Airex spinning reel, fit over the forefinger, thumb and part of the hand. When the mechanism was activated by a pneumatic switch or a throat microphone, it enabled the person wearing the hand to shave, eat, write, or type. Using George's design, John Pasciutti, another of Lionel's craftsmen, fashioned the first model of this aluminum "exo-skeleton glove."

For paralyzed individuals, this device offered hope that they could resume a few of the basic functions of daily living. Lionel asked George to demonstrate the hand, which Giaimo named the "Can-Do," at veterans hospitals and conventions of the American Medical Association in 1954 and 1955. Talk was heard at the firm of selling electric hands on a nonprofit basis to physical therapists and institutions. All sorts of publications rushed to tell about the inventions Giaimo had designed to make himself more mobile.

Once other engineers stepped in to oversee the production design of the hand, George started work on two challenging classified development contracts. He was pleased to be assisted by John Ferrer and Ted Stawski. With the three of them holed up in a separate laboratory at the plant, George paid little attention to what was going on with the electric hand.

So he was unprepared for the jolt soon to hit him. Lionel intended to patent the hand under Giaimo's name! George got wind of this when Lionel's patent attorney telephoned him and asked how the device worked. Perhaps someone at the firm's headquarters thought Giaimo deserved credit because the impetus for creating the hand had come from his physician. Maybe Giaimo insisted that, as works manager, he be recognized. Or sentiment that he'd endured so much as a paraplegic influenced the decision.

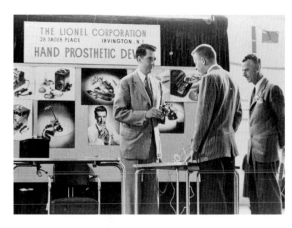

In June of 1955, Lionel dispatched George to San Francisco to demonstrate the electric hand for the American Medical Association.

Amazed and outraged, Vitt protested to the patent attorney, to no avail. Joe Bonanno ignored his appeal for assistance or at least an explanation.

"I lost respect for Giaimo and Bonanno," George comments. Once enthralled by his work on electric trains, military equipment, and a stereo camera, he now wanted out. Then a call to join Hughes Aircraft Co. Research Labs reached him in 1956. Without giving Lionel a chance to match the offer, he quit in September, packing up his things and heading for California. George stayed at Hughes, working in its Research Labs and Radar Systems Group until his retirement as Senior Scientist in 1989.

JUSTICE AT LAST

The years at Hughes were productive and enjoyable, although never in quite the same way as at Lionel. "I was younger then," George points out, "and the people left indelible marks on me." Over time, his indignation lessened. Justice was served in the early 1960s, after Giaimo had been let go and Bonanno was relieved of his duties, when George was officially asked to return as Lionel's chief engineer. The offer soothed his ego, but the sad state of affairs there led him to say no.

He's never regretted his decision. However, over the last decade, George has reestablished ties with old friends from Lionel. In addition to writing many letters, he's unpacked from his negative files the many rolls of film he shot and processed more than 40 years ago. His memories and photographs remind us that the company we associate with toy trains developed many other products that used electricity to influence life.